Wakefield Press

MAKING A STAND

After graduating from the University of Adelaide with an Honours degree in history, Erica Jolly taught in secondary schools for forty years, mainly in South Australian technical high schools until 1974. In 1978 she completed a Masters degree in English literature at Flinders University. Erica realised early that categorisation and predetermined pathways for students limited their scope and discouraged interdisciplinary approaches. In 1992 she gave up her position as Deputy Principal (Curriculum) at Marion High School. Elected to the Flinders University Council in 1990, she supported interdisciplinary developments. Her publications include social histories *We Came to Marion* (1995) and *A Broader Vision* (2001), a collection of poetry, *Pomegranates* (2003), and a book linking science and poetry, *Challenging the Divide* (2010).

Maureen Prichard is an artist, illustrator, lettering artist, writer and sometime art educator. Her practice is heavily informed by her research interests in mediaeval manuscripts and the design and illustration of private press books from the late nineteenth and early twentieth centuries. As a result her oeuvre centres on book illustration and decoration, and investigations into the image-text relationship in which hand lettering plays an important role. She has illustrated and designed over fifty books and book jackets for numerous Australian publishers.

Also by Erica Jolly

We Came to Marion

A Broader Vision

Pomegranates

Challenging the Divide

Maureen Prichard's illustrations to the poems were executed on scraperboard, their measurements and proportions derived from the first eight numbers of the Fibonacci sequence.

Making a Stand

Poems

Erica Jolly

Wakefield Press
16 Rose Street
Mile End
South Australia 5031

First published May 2015
Reprinted 2025

Text and cover designed and typeset by Michael Deves
Illustrations by Maureen Prichard

ISBN 978 1 74305 382 9

A catalogue record for this book is available from the National Library of Australia

Wakefield Press thanks Coriole Vineyards for continued support

I acknowledge that I live on the land of the Kaurna people, the traditional owners and custodians of what we now call the Adelaide Plains

Dedicated to

Eric Pfitzner

Hugh Stretton

Humphrey Tranter

Denis Grundy

Each of these men contributed in significant but intangible ways to my education.

And it is time my mother received the acknowledgement due to her for her role in my education.

Dorothy Woolford Jolly

[1897–1984]

Contents

No POEM
IN A RAIN PATTERN

Preface

Jennifer Strauss

'Poets', says Erica Jolly, 'find their themes in what matters to them', and a reader will discover quickly enough the things that matter – deeply and passionately – to this outspoken poet: rejection of the abuse of power; justice for the dispossessed, the brutalised, the impoverished; respect for the true matching of word to deed; an education that is holistic (no time for Gradgrindery here); a sense of wonder at her inhabited world in all its grandeur and its ordinariness. In a poem like 'Captured by the wonder of it all', she might well be seen as fulfilling the injunction 'Let not the sense of wonder die', spoken half a century earlier by Mary Gilmore, another outspoken woman with whom she has many affinities.

What we need to discern, however, is how intimately these things are interconnected for Erica Jolly and how much she is concerned at the ways in which losing the connectedness of the fabric of experience diminishes us as human beings. What matters above all for her is the interconnectedness of all the elements that make us human, creatures at once of brain *and* heart, sensibility *and* sense, not to mention material flesh.

This passage from E.M. Forster, who figures with Primo Levi as a type of the connected being in 'A cautionary tale about schooling in Australia', might well stand as an epigraph to *Making a Stand*:

> Only connect! That was the whole of her sermon. Only connect the prose and the passion, and both will be exalted, and human love will be seen at its height. Live in fragments no longer. Only connect, and the beast and the monk, robbed of the isolation that is life to either, will die. (*Howards End*)

And when Cyril Connolly writes in *Enemies of Promise* that 'much of [Forster's] art consists in the plain-ness of his writing, for he is certain of the truth of his convictions and the force of his emotions', the description could as well have been penned for Jolly. For her poetry does have a plain-ness of surface, a directness of address that is too confident of the urgency of what she must say to want to obscure its statement with over-decoration or distorted syntax. Her idea of the poet's *particular* capacity can be seen in these lines about three responses to an art installation:

> Three friends consider the form.
> The biologist sees vertebrae of dinosaurs.
> The mathematician is enthralled by wave motion.
> The poet takes in the connections.

And her role as poet is to express these connections, especially to defend those that are denied. For her, the denial of connection between science and the humanities is a battle to be fought with all the force of her poetry. One strategy is insistence on the emotional life involved in the sciences – note that the mathematician is 'enthralled' in the lines above. If scientists do forget their humanity, they will draw her indignation for perverting connection, as in 'A Scientist's Spinoza'

> A robot kept on a sterile bench
> waits in a laboratory in Canada.
>
> Why does it matter that scientists
> have named this thing Spinoza?
>
> . . .
> With God and Nature one, the philosophy
> of this outcast Jew fed Goethe's poetry.
>
> I came to love him in my post-war way. So
> now it stings that he should be reduced to
>
> a thing of metal being taught to play soccer -
> an experiment in artificial intelligence.

In similar vein, she asks indignantly whether 'far from nature' is to be 'the future technology offers'.

If indignation is a tone heard often here, it is the flip side of her positive sense of what should be celebrated. It is directed with crusading vigour against ignorance cultivated where knowledge should prevail, as when she castigates the 'merchants of doubt' who deny climate change; against weasel words that defile the proper relation between truth and language ('Time to reflect on core promises'); against Ministers of Education who cannot or will not understand the value of interdisciplinary studies ('What has sustainability to do with mathematics?'); against the indignities inflicted by the rich and powerful on the vulnerable.

I would not wish to make her poetry sound too heavy: some of it is quirky and funny. Nor would I want to suggest that content matters at the expense of art. Jolly's use of stanzaic form to give structure to her poems deserves to be noticed, but my time is limited and I would like to finish this Preface by quoting one poem in its entirety. I have chosen it because it seems to me typical of so much of Erica's work: its six-line stanzas express the need to make a stand, the inability to be silent when her sense of justice is assailed, the sense that the intelligence of the heart must get to work to correct the excesses of the intellect, because those excesses are abroad in the world, intruding into and threatening the world of modest sensory pleasure and human sociability that's evoked in the opening stanza. The poem exemplifies too the way that ideas exist in her work not as abstractions, but as experiences, felt in the pulse of the blood.

'Conversation at Lucia's'

Remembering Descartes' dictum 'je pense donc je suis' or
'Cogito ergo sum' ['I think therefore I am.']

Here, where aromas, perfumes test and tempt the senses
where shoppers come with wheeled wire baskets, walking frames
walking sticks, back packs, eco-friendly bags and children
in prams, on thighs, in arms, on shoulders, piggy-backed or
held by the hand – happy, contented, tearful or tired –
here, where we sip coffee and chat, he makes it clear.

Here, I feel it – feel that touchstone on the pulse –
know I must attack that so convenient separation
of mind from flesh, head from hand, intellect from
senses, ideas from consequences, so convenient
now for the more than three hundred long years
that men –well mainly men – have played that game.

He reminds me when he speaks of Jaime Guzman
Professor of Law at the Catholic University of Chile,
proud of his support for Pinochet – Franco's protegé –
proud it was his mind, his conception that laid down
the structure, the intellectual framework for this
secretive, cruel US-backed, ruthless regime.

So proud, in his safe intellectual tower, he
felt none of the pain, had no electrodes put
to his testicles, smelt none of the faeces,
heard none of the moans and screams of
those reduced by rape, saw none of the blood
tasted none of the grief in mothers' tears.

Jaime Guzman was proud – doing God's work –
raised by his intellect above the common herd
protected by that separation – his mind free
to act with impunity – he had no need to
feel what his laws might mean for those
who cried for mercy on the ground.

It's called the Cartesian principle –
that proof of who I am is in the power
of thought alone – safe from the
senses, feelings, hopes, fears and
consequences – and it has protected
Descartes' disciples for far too long.

Making a Stand

Introduction

Michael Cathcart, the host of the ABC Radio National's 'Books and Arts Daily' gave me this title. He was talking to a woman who had reviewed the work of a new Australian novelist. Discussing the novelist's approach, she suggested to Michael that he did not approve of didactic work. His reaction was immediate. He did not reject didactic writing. What he disliked, he said, was ambiguity. He wanted people to take a stand. I decided to title this collection 'Making a Stand'.

I was not happy when we lost 'The Book Show', the ABC's long-running Radio National program on writing and writers. In Ramona Koval's program there was no cultural divide, no impassable barrier between the sciences and the humanities. Given my preoccupation with the destructive impact of the idea of two irreconcilable cultures with science on one side and the humanities and the arts on the other, 'The Book Show' had been special for me.

Working with a group at the University of the Third Age on poetry and science, her fine program gave me the information that supported my view that these connections matter if we are to have the scientifically literate citizenry needed to build a better future for Australia's grandchildren.*

So it took me a while to accept the value of the replacement program, 'Books and Arts Daily'. However, this program would give me another justification for the stance I am taking. A woman interviewing the late Maya Angelou, the great American poet whose poetry was called 'black, bitter and beautiful' by James Baldwin, asked if she was a political poet.

Purists dismiss engagement with politics as merely polemics, as if such engagement reduces the art and beauty of poetry. Once the purists were against consideration of the environment. That was too political for them. Judith Wright would be caught up in that limitation by those who would have preferred her not to have written 'Australia 1970'. In that poem this great poet felt such outrage, she dared to try to make us see that we were [and I think still are] 'self-poisoners'.

I sat there listening and cheering. The answer Maya Angelou gave her interviewer was exactly what I needed to hear. She saw us all engaged in the political life of our place and time. In her place and time she was a poet. Politics, as part of her world, had a place in her poetry. She was asserting her right to be involved, as a poet, in whatever mattered to her. I now had another reason to thank Michael Cathcart.

Poets find their themes in what matters to them. How they approach it, how they interpret it depends on so many things. But in the process, as in so much else, they are learning. Just as I began to learn about the devastating effect of that notion of the 'great divide' (that supposedly irreconcilable division in C.P. Snow's *The Two Cultures*) while I was teaching in England in 1966/1967.

I have written about my discovery of the origins of the notion of the 'chasm' between the sciences and humanities in my introduction to *Challenging the Divide: Approaches to science and poetry* with its contributions by scientists and poets who refuse to be boxed in. Here I want to direct readers to C.P. Snow's *Second Look* in 1964 at the address called *The Two Cultures* given in Cambridge in 1959. By 1964 he had realised how destructive was the polarisation of the 'cultures'. Its impact in schools in the separation of students so early in their secondary schooling into this or that category had made it impossible for society to 'think with wisdom'.

Considering the problem of disconnection I thought about

people who insist they are non-political. And my mind went to sleep that 'knits up the ravelled sleeve of care'. I wondered if any of them had ever thought about where other people might sleep. Do they fear phosphorus or chlorine gas bombs dropped on them? Are they asylum seekers dumped in Nauru or on Manus Island? Are they exposed on a mountainside? Are their children weeping? Are they anxious about getting to that Centrelink appointment on time, possibly fearing the way they will be punished if a child demands attention and makes them late? Are their shares going down? Do they fear the unpredictable behaviour of a partner? Are they as lucky as I have been so far in what this new conservative Australian Prime Minister called 'the lottery of life' in 2013? Are they the unlucky ones threatened with job loss by this Prime Minister's spurious focus on 'efficiency dividends'? What attitudes, concerns, health problems go to bed with them? Remember Mr Ruddock, Minister for Immigration and Multi-cultural affairs in the Howard government from 1996–2003? He saw sleep deprivation as a legitimate way to extract information from suspects. In recent years the significance of the quality of sleep for the quality of our life has scientists engaged in studies of sleep patterns and insomnia.

Take any human need and ask the same questions. Even those in this nation now totally committed to the cult of selfishness with its focus on individualism, described so well by Hugh Stretton in 1987 in the essay where he shows how it is 'cultivated', might be forced to pause and consider that there might be social consequences they cannot evade. Even those among us following that appalling 'I'm all right, Jack' path might, in the future, need those connections they now despise and reject. It will be too late then. But I expect they believe their gamble will pay off. I expect they believe they do not need to learn. They will be safe.

Education, and the learning that comes with it, enters our homes in many informal ways. Often it is brought to us through the work of so many in the ABC: producers, presenters, researchers, documentary makers, composers, producers of drama and film, technicians have certainly been influential in my life. They have certainly had a vital role helping me become more aware of connections between the sciences, arts and humanities.

Writing at my kitchen table, I was listening to Australia's premier science broadcaster, Robyn Williams, on Radio National's forty-year-old 'Science Show'. He had just brought back to me the voice of Naomi Oreskes. A former mining engineer who had worked in South Australia, she has, with Erik M. Conway, just published a novel *The Collapse of Western Civilization*. They had collaborated before. Their book, *Merchants of Doubt* tackled the lies and deliberate misinformation of those who 'obscured the truth on issues of tobacco smoking and global warming'. Among those 'merchants' are those who have called climate change crap. Oreskes and Conway have knowledge and a social conscience. They know we need quality information if we are to be able to contribute as educated active citizens to a better future for all of us. They contribute to our education,

However, some scientists choose to have nothing to do with how the 'others', those on the other side of that so-called cultural divide, deal with the information they provide. Of course there are facts. For example the formula H_2O is a fact. It is a fact that two atoms of hydrogen combine with one atom of oxygen to make water. But the moment we think of it as water, it enters the broader arena. What do we do with water? Are we happy companies have leases on natural springs to sell water in bottles? What of the water supply in ground water? What of our artesian basins? Why is water essential in our lives? What of the future if we spend our time here as sleep walkers?

I could take examples from the periodic table. Whatever the element, if I chose, I could bring to this introduction 'the element of surprise' that I find in *Nature's Building Blocks* where John Emsley takes me to human elements: history, the role of an element in war, in medicine, in economics, in environment, in food. Education does not begin and end in a formal setting. Schooling might but education does not.

Learning begins so early in our lives. 'The Argonauts' were in mine very early, just as 'Play School' has been in the lives of so many since television was added to the world of radio. Opportunities for learning can come in play, can come through access to libraries, art galleries, the range of arts, music, film, theatre, through performances of all kinds, in zoos, botanical gardens, in nature with its complexity, engagement with different technology and instruments, through the wonder in beauty and in discovery of all kinds. And these opportunities as well can come to us through universities and TAFEs where face-to-face engagement invites exchange of ideas, fostering connections across cultures, connecting head, hand and heart through the enthusiasm and knowledge of those who engage with us.

The vulnerability of many of these avenues of learning can be demonstrated in part by the action of the Minister for Communications, Malcolm Turnbull, who has decided to destroy community radio and community television so he can sell off that waveband. Think also of small presses – Magabala Books for example – and street magazines offering alternatives to big commercial media. Informal avenues of learning like these can be central. They need to be protected and they can have a place in poetry if the poet so desires.

So many poets bring us a feeling for and understanding of some aspect of life that resonates with us. And it stays with us. It is not something to be afraid of. It is not something to dismiss as Richard Dawkins dismissed Keats' poem 'Lamia'. Keats' concern that the science of his time might be so mechanistic it had no place for the human spirit might give us pause today.

It is the job of poets to share with us their thoughts and feelings, to waken our senses and open our eyes, ears, minds, hearts. A poet might share his delight in a crane lifting cement walls for a building. Another might share his pleasure in the failure of the Colonels in Greece to impose their will on a festival at Epidauros in the 1970s. A South Australian poet in *Magic Logic* in a poem 'Reflection' might remind a mathematician his or her world is real. Shelley's poem 'The Cloud' contains the science of his time. Pope's 'Essay on Man' questions the way England is going in the early eighteenth century. Mark O'Connor's *Pilbara* brings the prose description of the place and the poem to face one another. A scientist and poet in *Urban Biology* takes us into the living memory of Mary Docherty, Edinburgh, 1828, the last victim of Burke and Hare who procured fresh bodies for the Edinburgh School of Anatomy.

Poets have tried to cross that 'two cultures' barrier. In 2010 the then Poets' Union Inc. joined the Science Made Marvellous program for National Science Week. Three volumes of poems by Australian poets were produced. *Holding Patterns: Physics and Engineering poems* was one. (My poem 'Sculpture at Questacon' was in it.) Next was *Earthly Matters: Biology and Geology poems*. Then *Law and Impulse: Mathematics and Chemistry poems*. The Royal Institution in the Science Exchange (RiAus) in Adelaide holds annual sci-ku competitions.

In 1964, answering those who thought he approved of that separation Snow wrote: '*There is no excuse for letting another generation be as vastly ignorant, or as devoid of understanding and sympathy, as we are ourselves.*' That was where we were. In 2015 probably it still is where we are. Our focus on science, technology, engineering and mathematics without considering the human context means we have a way to go to create the interdisciplinary, connected world we need. That is where Australia's Chief Scientist, Professor Ian Chubb, wants us to be. 'In the same tent'.

Ending on a more encouraging note, I recently listened to Robyn Williams talking to Lisa Jardine, daughter of Jacob Bronowski at the Festival of Science in Birmingham. He asked her if we had begun to make the lateral moves to close the gap between the cultures? She thinks the young have begun closing the gap. She wants all of us to share our gifts and our talents.

Erica Jolly
May 2015

* On Monday, 15 September 2014, on Q & A, we heard the Chief Scientist, Professor Ian Chubb, Dr Marita Chung, 2012 Young Australian Scientist of the Year, Professor Suzanne Cory, presenter of the 2014 Boyer Lectures, Nobel Prize Laureate immunologist Professor Peter Doherty and Nobel Prize Laureate astro-physicist, Professor Brian Schmidt.

References

John Emsley *Nature's Building Blocks: An A-Z Guide to the Elements*, Oxford, 2001.

C.P. Snow *The Two Cultures and a Second Look*, Cambridge, 1964.

Hugh Stretton 'The Cult of Selfishness' in *Political Essays*, Georgian House, Melbourne, 1987.

MUSIC TUNED TO MIDDLE C FOR A SPECIAL BEE

Judy Morris's Wollemi Pine

Nine panels covered with pencil: three panels purely pencil, the other six printed in colour from digital images before graphite pencil or black and white pastel has been drawn over printed colour for shadows and tonal range. The work of artist and scientist Judy Morris.

Something brings me back
to the core of that Wollemi Pine
where, almost lost in leaves
it sits in the central panel.

Around it, above, beside, below
the softest blue-green leaves
branching, drooping from
bending stems of trunks.

At the heart of the work
infinitesimal, growing at
a node, the tiniest buds
arouse my curiosity.

Such a minute cluster –
I'm told it is the polar cap.
A polar cap? I think of ice floes,
ice bergs, frozen landscapes.

Returning to the mystery
each time I discover a little more –
this cluster kept this conifer
alive throughout millennia.

Thick, waxy, its surface saving them
from the power of those ice ages
terminating the *Araucariaceae*
of the northern hemisphere.

South of the equator this family
of great pines thrived until other plants
with more adaptive flowering habits
began to take their place.

A mere thirty million years ago
they were flourishing here in Gondwana –
until climate change threatened and
and took their habitat from them.

Or so it seemed – but in a canyon
deep and hidden, safe from freezing ice
and human depredation, this pine with
its separate trunks would survive.

Reading a T-shirt advocating 'Slow School'

It's time to pause
take in the wonder
of thickened leaves
turning their edges
to the sun to
save water.

It's time to explore
mosaics and shapes of
green leaves adapted
to bring sunlight
to their surfaces
to feed the tree.

It's time to pause
consider the changes
with buds opening on
freezing mid-winter days
Lorraine Lee perfume
delighting a cold nose.

Captured by the wonder of it all

Enthralled by the documentary produced by BBC Scotland and shown on Australia's great ABC How to Grow a Planet

Was it a mere one hundred and forty million years ago
when light, harnessed from our star, colonised the land

when those leaves of *Amborella trichopeda* in
New Caledonia mutated to form flowers on stems

tiny creamy flowers attracting early beetles
so pollen began to stick to these couriers?

How did they survive when landscapes changed
and deserts replaced great stands of conifers

and ferns relying on the spread of sperm
by wind or water? Did flowers have seeds in cells

seeds that, in whatever soil, hard or sand
might hold on, germinate and offer food?

How did they survive if couriers disappeared?
When did they find that scatter-gun approach

the power they developed to eject seeds to
ensure some survived to lift shoots to the light?

And what of flowers offering brilliant colours –
one with music tuned to middle C for a special bee.

All this so many millennia ago, taking time
so much time as landscapes changed again

until grasses, fed by fire, could replace flowers
and bring to herbivores grain in place of fruit.

And we are left with the vision of homo sapiens
domesticating wheat, freeing us to ignore this past

freeing us, in our cities, not to think of this wonder –
allowing us to kill those couriers with pesticides.

Here, in my backyard, with minute buds along
stems of exotic fiddlewood becoming flowers

and a native paper bark with its cream-coloured
bottlebrush out there calling, bees have not yet come.
Why are these couriers slow to answer their call?

Honeybees

She watches them drinking
all of them sipping in a circle
around the edge of the dish.

They know it is getting hotter.
Their first responsibility is to
the queen, the hive, the future.

No time to shift pollen from
anthers on stamen to stigma
to let fertilisation take place.

Each hive must be kept safe.
The water they collect must
go home to keep them cool.

No time to follow bee lines
into the heart of a bloom for
nectar if a hive is in danger.

She watches, enthralled by
this knowledge in Nature
brought to her by the bees.

They know, instinctively,
when temperature will rise
or when it is likely to fall.

****

Photographs on a computer
bring me the evidence of bees
millions of bees lying there
dying beneath their hives.

What is this? Companies,
rich chemical companies are
suing the EU council for
daring to pass laws to
protect bees from
their pesticides.

* * * *

In New York, a corporation,
looking beyond this planet
caring nothing about bees
with no interest in anthers
stigma, ovaries, nectaries
the honey they make or
fruit they help to grow,
has taken their name
to make money from
machines out in space
& they call themselves
Honeybee Robotics.

'What has sustainability got to do with mathematics?'

An exclamation attacking interdisciplinary themes in the national curriculum by Christopher Pyne on Q & A, *28 October 2013*

Does he not know or care
humankind must measure?

Does he not know or care
PhDs in applied mathematics

are measuring ground water levels
recording changes over time?

Does he not know or care
artesian reserves are crucial?

Does he not know or care
we measure temperature each day

to check the impact of heat
or wind or rain on flood or fire?

Does he not know or care
why we measure soil quality?

Will this Minister of Education
ever open his mind to connections?

In praise of adventitious roots

Provoked by the Chair of the Australian Curriculum and Reporting Authority – ACARA – who dared to tell me that interdisciplinary study is cheap, lazy and shallow

Where would we be without those shallow roots
anchoring those plants – grasses filling fields,
wide-spread plains – savannahs, prairies, pampas
meadows – feeding herds of great kangaroos,
bison, deer, antelopes grazing ancient estates?

Where would we be today without those roots
of barley, wheat, rice, maize providing seeds
to be pounded by women, turned to flour
made into the stuff of life when fire, tamed,
baked clay turning dough into bread?

Where would we be without shallow roots
underground fuelling stems, buds, flowers, seeds
taking in mineral salts, water and sometimes
nitrogen, meeting all those essential needs
academics forget when they use that word?

Fleurieu Peninsula

Some seek the key to healing sleep
in your quiet winter green curves.

You seem to invite pillowed rest
for work-worn minds and hearts.

My friend sees lovers' shapes
moving beneath cloudy sheets.

Looking at 'Fourteen pieces' on North Terrace

An installation by Angela and Hossain Valamanesh in front of the South Australian Museum

Magpie larks perch, dip beaks and drink.

Children finger the surface, making ripples.

Mothers laugh, smile at quiet reflections.

Smooth surface sparkles in summer light.

Gravity draws water down rough grooves.

Algae grab hold bringing life to granite.

Three friends consider the form.

The biologist sees vertebrae of dinosaurs.

The mathematician is enthralled by wave motion.

The poet takes in the connections.

What have they done to the Waterhouse Art Prize at the South Australian Museum?

For a decade
natural history
has been revealed
in works of art.

Sculptures of ants
fresh water eels
there in oil on wood
and 'Nature's lace'.

Bush plums dotted
in acrylic on linen –
the Ediacara suite of
our Flinders Ranges.

Stories stare at us
of life through time
sometimes in glass
perhaps in porcelain.

For a proud decade
they kept to tradition
with that adjective and
that common noun.

No fear of connecting
our natural world with
visions of our earth
even with poetry.

No desire to cut off
knowledge of nature
in all those millennia
from our humanity.

But history for some
belongs over there on
the other side of that
man-made divide.

No poem in a rain pattern.
They've changed the title.
History and poetry will not
intrude again on *science*.

A way to view the future

Acknowledging Lewis Thomas author of The lives of a cell

Elements of me will be
in billions, trillions
of atoms here, there
somewhere in space-time.

Perhaps part of the
music of the spheres
a crochet, a quaver
a larynx, diaphragm
vibrating somewhere
past, future, now.

Perhaps caught in amethyst
lost in lavender or lilac
sloughed off skin
inhaled by lady bird –
somewhere, anywhere
content to be unaware.

Caught in a bind

They stop me short
heavy wings flapping
voices harsh and loud
above in the yard.

Small birds fly higher
eager to outstrip danger
from that trio of great
black marauding crows.

Metal sounds behind me
from the galvanised fence
make me turn to find
a new, different bird.

Softer, a mottled brown
a broader back he or she
teeters there while crows
stalk on the next-door roof

It turns. I see the broad face.
go back to Stratford and
recall an owl in silent flight.
I want to keep her safe.

Sharp beaks, sharp eyes
crows watch while she hides.
I move so she must decide
which danger is worse.

Her claws are uneasy on
that cutting iron edge. Which
is worse? Danger out there
or behind? She decides to fly.

In *All's Well that Ends Well* the challenge of the new

Shakespeare would draw in the groundlings
bring them into the great debate between
the past, the present and the future.

And in this play, this later comedy
he would present the future through
the courage of a young woman.

Old schoolmen, august physicians
imbued with the precepts of Aristotle
had told His Majesty there was no hope.

Bedridden, in agony with his fistula
the King of France had been advised
to prepare his soul for that dread event.

A young woman, orphaned, daughter
of a renowned physician, trusted by him
would bring his remedy to the court.

Offering her sovereign her father's cure,
prepared to lose her life if she should fail,
she dared him to try this experiment.

But, in the king's cries 'No empirics'
I would hear the power of the past,
the fear of the future, the fear of change.

* * * *

Centuries on and in my ear empirics
is not a dirty word – I hear no abuse –
no untrained practitioner, no quack.

Centuries on that word has a place
in scientific discourse – empiricism is
investigation based on observation.

Brought to this discovery through
my dictionary of the roots of words
I'm aware this term has lost its taint.

In *Novum Organum*, Bacon's reply
to Aristotle's rules of logic this word
gains respectability, changes its use.

In that new beginning, that revolution in
scientific thinking, 'empirics' is not a quack
no longer just an untrained practitioner.

* * * *

For the dying king, her gamble, her readiness
to die if she should fail, makes him take the risk
accept the gamble – what does he have to lose?

If she, this young girl, sure in her knowledge
can get him out of bed, give him life again
he will try this remedy – and pay her well.

And she does. And he does. Although her price
is the right to have for her husband the man
she loves whether he wants her or not.

While love and war fill the rest of the play,
there, for me, in 'No empirics' is a catalyst –
a catalyst showing the readiness of Shakespeare
to prepare his audience for the changes of his time.

Note: *All's Well that Ends Well* was probably presented at the Globe in 1604 or 1605
Francis Bacon's *Novum Organum* was published in 1620.

Michael's Cage

Thinking of the scientist and artist, Judy Morris, in her work in charcoal and white pastel

Michael Faraday
invented this cage
173 years ago to protect
his scientific research from
forces beyond his control.

I am back with that young man
the son of poor but loving parents
who gave him the basics they could afford
and the spiritual strength to find his way,
to take his chance when it came
ignore the snobbery and derision
of a woman determined to
keep him in his place.

He could wait his turn, work,
rise above black balling
by a jealous scientist
who would keep him down
and when he had the chance
light a candle to curiosity
and share with children
his delight in discovery.

Today he is here
in the loving soft grey depths
of charcoal and white pastel
in the bits and pieces
made by other hands
for the same purpose –
uncovering the unknown.

Sculpture at Questacon

Poetry and science

It looks like magic –
children are turning
a great stone sphere
this way and that
smoothly, easily.

Girls and boys are
moving this sunlit
glistening ball
floating above its base

laughing, splashing
delighting in their power
to change the direction
of this massive globe.

But it is not magic –
it is mathematics
and imagination
and water engineered
to raise solid granite.

From the classics through chance to chemistry and beyond

Quotations from Primo Levi's comments on 'To See Atoms' one of the lectures chosen by Primo Levi when he set out on his 'Search for Roots': A Personal Anthology – *his essential reading – the thirty pieces of prose and poetry he chose for this book that was translated into English by Peter Forbes*

At the age of sixteen a student
the youngest, smallest, cleverest
and the only Jew in this class
is studying the classics.

And no wonder, for the son of
a liberal Jewish Turin family in
Mussolini's Italy might uncover
much in the story of ancient Rome

among poets, writers, historians
perhaps Virgil, Caesar, Seneca
even the work of the poet Lucretius
even *De Rerum Natura.*

And in 1935 he finds in lectures
perhaps in a library – call it chance –
in English, *Concerning the nature of things,*
Lucretius's poem about the Greek atomists

lectures given by a Nobel prize winner –
once the Elder Professor of Mathematics
who taught far from Europe's centres of science
and found joy in life and physics in Adelaide.

Sir William Bragg had delivered them
in 1925 at the Royal Institution.
A decade on, Bragg's words in 'To see atoms'
offer this boy a way to explore the universe.

He is 'captivated by the clear and
simple things that they say' – 'divining' in
Bragg's vision 'a great hope' moving from
'the world of minute atoms' . . . 'infinitely far'.

He decides to be a chemist and again –
with chance on his side – this student
matriculates and enters university
just before Jews are denied that right.

Chemistry will save him from German hands.
He is of value, worth keeping alive.
The SS in Auschwitz can use this chemist
to make synthetic rubber for their industries.

When he catches scarlet fever, fear of contagion
makes his guards isolate him in the sanatorium
where he lies while his compatriots are marched
to their death before the Russians arrive.

Auschwitz becomes the catalyst –
a writer and a poet comes back to Italy
ready to make all who would rather forget
feel and face their part in this genocide.

In different stories, in *The Periodic Table*,
chemist and story teller combine elements
in narrative for us – the general readers –
giving us the human connection we need.

Before he dies, in *The Search for Roots*,
he leaves us a legacy of four pathways and
there is his conviction that William Bragg,
with Lucretius, Darwin and Clarke, belongs
on the pathway of 'salvation through knowledge.'

Humanity in science

Based on Chemistry Imagined: reflections on science *by Roald Hoffmann and Vivian Torrence published by Smithsonian Institution Press 1993*

Because I do not see them
does not mean they are not there
nor that I am not made of them

this quantum chemist
poet and playwright
will help me to learn

to go beneath the skin
discover the stories of
molecules and elements

because this fine teacher
moves beyond the abstract
to delight in my world

inhabited by people
who laugh cry write
search struggle find

feels the soldiers choking
gives to science students
'Dulce et decorum est'.

The BBC Scotland Science Unit has done it again

First How to Grow a Planet, *now* The Secret Life of the Sun

This time, women with men, solar physicists
their language so clear taking us into
the furnace of our local star showing
us just how, in that centre, sunlight
is born in fusion, taking aeons to
reach through heated plasma
to the surface where, free
at last, the photons
bring us light.

This time, with women and men playing the game,
they compare the movement of particles to
pin balls making their way past barriers
while photons face magnetic fields.
The story begins with a total eclipse
and a corona seen in Queensland,
a corona, a halo with the sun
at its maximum preparing
to bring us in this cycle
solar winds, weather
and those lights

those green Northern Lights reminders
of the power of wonder, the curiosity
the desire to see, the itch to learn
and learning, take command.
Galileo, writing sonnets in
Petrarchan mode, first
saw the sun spots
asked what they
could mean
for us.

This time, women with men,
now equals in investigation
trying now to create fusion
in great laboratories with
laser beams so powerful
they stagger the mind.
Women tell this tale
show us the veil
between us and
the solar winds.

Visiting 'Not Absolute'

An exhibition in the Flinders City Gallery part of the SA Living Arts Festival (SALA) engaging the sciences and the arts

There is no chasm here insisting on separation
no great divide assuming one is either this or that.

Here humanity comes first in these works of art
by scientists, researchers who have loved their life

bringing their love, knowledge, understandings
and imagination to share their excitement with us

who once were taught as others still are told
they might be one or the other, not both.

In 'Twelve Hours of Breath', half a day's breathing
captured for us to see how much the artist takes in

and, blown in molten glass, bubbles of shorter breaths
transparent, elliptical, curtailed, speak of life's brevity.

There is no fear here – feelings, thought, ideas, craft –
shared, discussed, realised and brought forth in art

take our understanding of ourselves, of one another
just that little bit further – connecting the arts and
sciences.

After visiting the Darwin Centre of the Natural History Museum in London, October 2013

Come with me. Take the glass-walled lift
to the Cocoon up here on Level Seven.
Accept the invitation. Enter this shelter,
this long curved protected space
comfortable and quiet where one
can take one's time, learn
and grow.

We are welcomed by a woman –
the curator of arachnids
in the David Attenborough studio –
who in this visual electronic image
invites us to walk along
the downward slope, to
take our time, to stop
touch buttons to meet
her other colleagues –
members of the team.

This time a young woman
a scientist from Colombia
in love with butterflies
researching this species
offering us the pleasure
of her company until
we decide to walk on.

Another alcove – this time an historian.
He will introduce men and a woman
whose contributions to natural history
demand consideration. First
it's Joseph Banks for me.

Not Banksia this time. Breadfruit
and an historian from the Caribbean
making clear his indifference
to humanity. Breadfruit fed
slaves to profit the Empire
in the West Indies.

Then Evelyn Cheesman in love with life –
as a woman denied the right to be a vet
turning to natural history, unafraid
trusted by people in New Guinea
discovering species on her own
throughout the South Pacific.

On the walls glowing images speaking of diversity.
We move along and down, bringing to light
with the touch of a button, biologists,
geneticists. Later a display of articles
taken by researchers to the field.
Among them a well-thumbed
War and Peace.

We are held in admiration of orchids
painted by artists on the curving wall,
stopped by windows letting us see
into their daily working lives.

Sitting in an alcove we listen to a scientist
giving us the details of the long
slow process of observation,
hypothesis, more observation
more collection, checking
amassing data, writing
presenting for review
rejection, correction
and one day, one year
perhaps acceptance.

Finally, in case we have not learned
in case we have been too blind to see
too impatient to move on, or
too deaf to hear, we are told.
This is the team – historian,
scientist, artist, curator.

This is the team – no segregation
of science from history. No desire
to turn natural history into
natural science. No desire
to remove history from
the stories of Nature.
No desire to restrict
all the forms of Nature
just to Science.

This is the essential team –
historian, scientist, artist, curator.

Here in this great Natural History Museum is
a way to feel the beating heart of learning.
And, if you have seen and heard, you will emerge
from this Cocoon, like me, quietly comforted.
At least here in London, these colleagues
are eager for us to learn, to grow with
the knowledge there should be, need be
no segregation of the cultures.

In the Earth Hall of the Natural History Museum of London

Acknowledging The Earth: An Intimate History *by Richard Fortey*

Geologically speaking this rock is gneiss (nis):
'a metamorphic rock composed, like granite, of
quartz, feldspar or orthoclase, and mica but
distanced from it by its foliate or laminated
structure.' (*Shorter Oxford Dictionary*)

* * * *

In that hall with each object speaking to me
of times long past, aeons ago, measured
by carbon dating to help us feel
the immensity in such numbers
beyond our comprehension

the great green curling forms of ammonites
the nodes so far apart in tall bamboos
the crinkled narrow ridges of giant clams
the solid trunk of tree turned to agate
and a rock 2,500 million years old.

Sliced vertically, the surface bright. Such vitality
in what seemed to me the magma caught
between strata, lifted, thrust down, now
still, the flow – pinkish white – halted
five hundred million years ago.

Was I being told the story of that dynamic fiery core
pushing up from the depths all that time before
bacteria formed in oceans so long before
that first move landward, in so much
thrusting, crushing, lifting motion?

What had brought this great movement to an end?
Fivc hundred million years ago it had stopped.
Another change elsewhere, another shift
this time of tectonic plates, bringing
to an end the wave motion that still
has me enthralled.

Discovering physics in old age

Darkening skin of pomegranates

Red touch of rust in Volkswagen

Eudora refusing to send e-mails

Entropy

Discovering more physics in old age

via Natalie Angier's Whirligig Tour of the Beautiful Basics of Science

So, this is why
I have no desire
to leave my bed
and test the air
each winter
morning.

Not laziness.
It's the negative
impact of these
infinitesimal
fragments of
the cosmos –
electrons!

A different kind of pie

After listening to 'Future Tense' on Radio National, 29 April 2012

Not apple, apricot or custard
not crumbled, no glazed crust
no need to count calories.

This 'pie' begins in Cambridge.
An electronic team provides
access to the digital world

to the poor, without funds
for the latest costly machine
outsourced to cheap labour.

Anywhere, here and there
attached to a television set
it lets students be creative.

Just an old one found on a tip,
a television set dumped there
will make all the difference.

For only twenty five dollars
boys and girls can become
the makers of programmes.

This pi, a letter of the
Greek alphabet – π –
comes with another fruit.

Raspberry Pi, now a Foundation,
helps young people to make
simple computers able to be
held in the palm of the hand.

Listening to a 'Shadow Catcher' on Radio National 10 June 2012

Jim Frazier says: 'Had I been a scientist,
I would never have made it.'

It all begins with spiders, too small for the camera's lens
too low down even for close attention to record their
stories.

It all begins with spiders and the desire to help friends
share with us their love of and delight in wild life.

If he can only find a way to get closer to their world
he might bring to us his fascination with its variety.

Scientists are discouraging and disparaging. They know
the inverse square law, the equation one over 'd' squared.

Just as Newtonians knew Faraday's field theory could not
work,
they know his law of optics and light will not allow it.

He will find a way with a staggered lens and adaptations
to magnify, make it possible to be there capturing the
moment.

Spielberg and David Attenborough will use his lens
bring us the broadest sweep and most minute on film.

It will take six million dollars from American film
companies
to do him down in courts, deny him the reward of his
labours.

But this shadow catcher, this Australian outsider, is not
defeated.
He has the Frazier Ultimate Two in his sights and with it
an acronym.

A Scientist's Spinoza

A robot kept on a sterile bench
waits in a laboratory in Canada.

Why does it matter that scientists
have named this thing Spinoza?

A red covered book lies with those
piled on my bed head for night reading:

Baruch then his own Benedictus Spinoza
and men whose ideas materialised our world,

in another birthday present from
my mother in nineteen fifty-four.

She fed me ideas to keep me safe from
midnight scratches at the door by a scientist

whose hands I longed to feel cupping
my face, my breasts before he disappeared

into some safe Platonic realm where
Beethoven was a great mathematician.

So through *Makers of Modern Thought*
I sought to go where he seemed to lead.

Spinoza was a man – not a Latin tag –
no 'cogito ergo sum' for him – he worked.

He refused to sell his soul or mind and
dared defy the elders in the synagogue.

Eyes pored over texts on his dim-lit desk
beside the attic bench that held his tools.

Glass dust slowly rasped his lungs red raw
from lenses ground to keep his mind alive.

With God and Nature one, the philosophy
of this outcast Jew fed Goethe's poetry.

I came to love him in my post-war way. So
now it stings that he should be reduced to

a thing of metal being taught to play soccer –
an experiment in artificial intelligence.

Possibilities in three-dimensional printing

It's Qi and Stephen Fry.
On his curved bench a toy
a smaller model of the sea-beast
one can visit on a shore in
the Netherlands.

Brought into being by
3D printer, with seventy-two
moveable joints, as a much
larger beast, it walks
along the shore on
their side of the
Channel.

* * * *

It's the 7.30 Report and
a Texan, an anarchist wants
everyone to be able to print
his or her own 3D gun like
his. A gun with a trigger
or a gun that is bigger
that will fire bullets
to hit their targets.

* * * *

In small print *Cosmos* asked
'Can 3D printing solve the organ
donor shortage'? But their image
offered a different way to see
the possibilities in this
advanced machine.

With straight, synthetic, shining
waist-long blonde hair, a Barbie doll
with pale skin, breasts pointed up,
hips narrow, long slender thighs
arms moving, face empty
stiffly walked west.

Was this what Australia's journal of
'The Science of Everything' was offering us?
Was this what we would be expected to do
with this new bio-tech marvel?

Footnote: In 2014 the CSIRO used 3D printing to construct a titanium heel to save a man from having his leg amputated and we are being told by RiAus just what 4D printing might be able to do for us as far as housing is concerned.

Is this the future technology offers?

Acknowledging Shelley's poem 'The Cloud' and
The Cloud-Spotter's Guide *by Gavin Pretor-Pinney,*
Sceptre Paperback, 2007

Is this where I'm expected to live and have my being
bodiless, except for fingers on keys and eyes on the screen
the portal taking me out there into cyber space
where memory lies beyond the hyper realm
able, with a universal service bus,
to be plugged in or taken out?

How far is this beyond the 'nursling of the sky'
Shelley brought to this century in the poem
he based on the science of his time?

Is this where the future lies far from nature
in these virtual clouds, formless 'utilities'
far from cumulus glowing at sunrise
always looking down not skyward
blind to Cape York's 'morning glory'
to variety and the chance of rain?

Vapour Trails

Acknowledging Apollo's Fire: a day on earth in nature and imagination *by Michael Sims*

They appear in the southern sky
climbing high beyond the cirrus clouds
so cold, so far above the turning earth.

Called condensation trails
beyond the Equator – streaks of white
I follow them out of sight.

Artificial clouds
products of our need
to get there yesterday.

Thinking about the 'Goldilocks' planet

Scientists have said
our blue planet is
'Just right' for us.

But Goldilocks
came, ate, slept
broke chairs.

Today, we
might call it
home invasion.

And she left
careless of destruction
and distress.

Will she be
on the 'ship' that
leaves Earth behind?

Arrival by post

A sepia photograph on the front page
brings me these engineers' new toy.
Bald, eyes bright, thin lips, just the faintest smile
reminding me of 'Star Trek's' Patrick Stewart.
It's soon to be exhibited in Beijing.
They're proud it can write basic poetry.
It is called the thinking head and I wonder
if, one day, plugged in somewhere, it will mouth
Descartes' words 'Je pense, donc je suis.'

I hate gadgets but . . .

I hate gadgets
but because
I'm afraid to
miss a call
this machine
saves me from
slipping
sliding
standing
shivering
dripping
while
wet
hands
hold the
phone.

Instead
it can speak
capture the voice
and the red light
can blink while
I stay warm
lingering in
lavender foam
licking quince
from my
bottom
lip.

At the airport

In silhouette
a white-faced heron rests on barbed wire
setting its mark upon the world.

He mocks the heavier form
rising above that fence
hurling itself skyward.

Sharply etched –
at home on this grey day
he's free.

we have... no King Lear to remind us about the price a nation pays for blindness

Reading Kate Grenville's novel *The Secret River* in London

Her novel is dedicated to the Aboriginal people of Australia: past, present and future

What did the Jesuits say:
'Give me a child till he is seven
and I have him for life.'

Must that be true of a child
brought up on Arthur Mee
and the Round Table of Camelot

on the Norman Conquest at
Hastings, then Errol Flynn's
Robin Hood there in Sherwood

and King John made to kneel
accede to the will of his nobles
forced to sign the Magna Carta?

Must that be true of children
brought up on British history
in Australia's post war schools

when Britain was still 'home'
with Elizabethan glory renewed
when this was White Australia?

Seeing Boadicea and her daughters
in that great chariot still fighting
in bronze now opposite Westminster

seeing all those blue plaques on
houses, the statues – preserving history
in the weight of all that metal and stone

remembering all the books and words –
Peter Pan in Piccadilly – and Captain Cook
at Greenwich with other great sailors

bringing that belief in the superiority
of all they brought to Sydney Cove.
I feel the need to go beyond those stories.

Reading *The Secret River* in London
I feel the old urge so strongly as we travel
past memories down Old Father Thames

and I fear I understand why so many
of us have so little respect for spinifex
mallee, desert rose – land, rocks, trees

so little respect that we would rather go on
telling that story as our history, ignoring
the culture in all the life here before 1788.

I come home with that child in me but
also the adult I am becoming in the hope
others, caught in that time, are breaking free.

Listening to Tim Bowden's documentary on Radio National Summer, 2007

I cannot resist –
every morning at eleven o'clock
I stop work, leave the computer
come to sit beside the radio
not to miss a word of those old voices
women's voices, men's voices
taking me back to childhood
and other broadcasts about
Australians under Nippon.

They bring me stories of
prison camps and nightmares
that, even here safe in Adelaide
disturbed my young sleep.

Now I hear the voices
laughing finding irony
in memories too sad for tears
memories of market forces
put in place by Americans
who see a way to survive.
Sick men cannot eat –
they can sell their ration,
the buyer will repay with rice.

Entrepreneurs build their banks
demand payment from debtors
forced to give up a day's ration
bankrupt them to skin and bone.

I hear their wry laughter –
'The bankrupts hung out
with the Dutch pastor.
He ensured they had a bit
to eat, did deals with creditors
to repay rice in grain instalments,
got them to accept repayment
over time to let a debtor have
enough to stay alive.'

I hear that change in tone
love the decency in their story.
When the Aussies came
they heard the Yanks with their cries
of 'Rice for sale.' Some one said
'Give it away. We Aussies share with mates.
We don't sell food. That's not our way.'

But fifty years on I hear again and again,
in an Australia that says it wants us to honour
our fighting men, politicians, business men
bankers repeating 'Let market forces decide.'

So I wait for us to go the whole hog
decide, like those men, to privatise war for profit.

Night thoughts on a poetry workshop

I watch each deliberate movement –
note his care to match
the horizontal level
of each letter,

and the exactitude
with which he places
his favoured fountain pen
vertically on the page.

I listen to each considered reply –
hear each pause before speech
feel the judicious weight
he gives each word.

Should one write political poetry?
His verdict? 'On reflection, no.'
One should always wait –
he sees such work as rant.

In the dark I hear Wordsworth
pleading with Milton to come
'England hath need of thee,
She is a fen . . .'

Blake's 'mind-forged manacles'
clank in my brain and
I hear feet shuffling
in chains.

Shelley invokes that
cleansing wild west wind
so he might speak to
'unawakened earth.'

I come at last
to the skull of an ox
with food and coins
placed in its eye sockets

symbolic ritual
of human care for
all kinds of refugees
in Pablo Neruda's Chile.*

In this paper-bark dawn
with parrots feasting on blossom
I wake with an answer
to his reflection.

* From Pablo Neruda's Lecture after he was awarded the Nobel Prize for Literature, 13 December 1971

After watching *Q & A* on the Queen's Birthday 2011

With Merchants of Doubt *by Naomi Oreskes and Erik M. Conway, Bloomsbury Press New York, 2010, in mind*

Ring the bells. Wake up all the sleepers.
I've heard that word out of the mouth
of the woman with the double-barrelled surname
who could be Minister for the Ageing
if they were in power.

She's responding to a question
from a man challenging the
teaching of climate change
in our schools, a man who
calls gravity just a theory.

Should it be taught in science –
when it is only a theory?
She agrees. This is just a debate
and there must be balance
balance – equal time.

It is as if she knows the strategy
employed so well by so many
industries, businesses eager
to undermine the science
determined to sow doubt.

Backing their schemes with billions
they establish 'research Institutes'
to provide academic respectability
and pay often elite physicists
to broadcast their view.

And they are here – she has said the word –
balance – that deceptive appeal to reason by
big tobacco, by big electric men
who reject acid rain and by
coal and oil men, miners against
any anthropogenic impact of carbon.

Ring the bells, Wake all our sleep walkers.
Find a way, not in scientific journals
that only other scientists read. Maybe in
this International Year of Chemistry
we can sound the alarm and denounce
these merchants of doubt.

Thinking of Pablo Neruda's Legacy

I see him there denied the right to mourn
the death of his good friend in those last days.

Instead he must hear the tramp and shouts
of soldiers turning his garden upside down.

I see him lying there while Pinochet's men
destroy his peace by the sea that filled his poetry.

Here, on the other side of that Pacific Ocean
I read the story of this poet's resurrection.

He will be restored: 'Poetry will fall from the sky'
they say. 'There will be joy, laughter in carnival.'

But for me, in this land where we prefer war
I take in the words he spoke to his tormenters.

As they hunted for weapons in his grounds, he said
'The only weapons you will find in this place are words.'

Advertising *Lapham's Quarterly*

Volume 1, Number 1, Winter 2008 – 'States of War'

Surprise, surprise – a gift of sanity
from USA bringing me voices of
past and present finding noble reasons
for war. He wants us to think, take
in through the depths of human history
the soaring rhetoric of war.

We hear Achilles preparing for battle
'testing himself in all his gear',
hear boots tramping on the ground
and blood seeping into earth for years,
see a child soldier with his gun
sitting in an abandoned classroom.

We hear the orders to young boys in
Sparta 'Come back with your shield
or on it.' And Kant, a German philosopher
tells us 'There is no State whose Leader
does not wish to secure permanent peace
by conquering the universe.'

We hear Pope Urban II at Clermont
using every savage picture of evil –
rape, torture, tongues torn out
flogging till the 'viscera gushed forth'
to arouse believers to take the road,
to Jerusalem in the Crusades.

That warlike rhetoric, bypassing
thought, evidence as Voltaire said,
'of a deformed imagination', calling
for sacrifice by others, not the
money makers, not those profiting
from the chaos in life and death.

That rhetoric, so strong in the words of General Patton telling his troops, 'You are here because you are real men and all real men like to fight.' So 'Rip them up the belly.' and 'Shoot them in the guts.'

This American brings us the horror of that rhetoric with its capacity to turn us into mindless followers – 'Voices in Time', 'Calls to Arms', 'Rules of Engagement', 'Field Reports' and 'Post mortems'.

A startling comparison discovered while exploring the Melbourne Theatre Company website

The playwright David Williamson is speaking
about his latest play Rupert

He is comparing him
this media magnate
with Richard III.

He loves that play in which
a lesser being manages
to scale the heights.

Ruthless, cunning, sly
nothing and no one
gets in his way

Not homicidal –
our author, this playwright
is careful to say.

But in 1485 the White Boar
was forced to take real risks
had to take up arms himself.

Today a media monarch
need not dirty his hands when
words can do the work.

On Radio National Tuesday 6 June 2006

Remembering Anna Politkovskaya, courageous journalist, fighter for human rights, mother of Vera and Ilya

She speaks to me in Russian
with sharp rasping accents and
in the soft translator's voice,
I discover the reason.

This Russian journalist tells me
about that other leader in the 'war'
the so-called war on terror –
Putin, once Head of the KGB.

She has covered the war in Chechnya,
has seen men and women – whether
they are Russian or not – bombed,
killed as they lie on the ground.

She has dared to write all the stories
of those military signs on Federal camps
has smelt the urine and faeces excreted
in dead Grosny's city mosques.

'Islam is a disease and we are here
to cure it.' Cure it by the murder
of men who, wearing no underpants,
are still forced to drop their trousers.

She is telling us of those young women
in Chechnya, poisoned in experiments
now mentally deranged, made sterile
by Russians proceeding with their cure.

At the Sydney Writers' Festival she is risking
her life. She is bearing witness to the cruelty
of Russian punitive raids. Three months on
she will be assassinated as she leaves home.

You're not going to cry, are you?

No, I'm not going to cry
when I hear the word 'rendition'
changed this way.

No longer Ella Fitzgerald's rendition
of 'Night and Day'

or Frank Sinatra's interpretation
of 'I've Got You Under My Skin'

or Shirley Bassey's approach
to 'I Get a Kick Out of You'.

No, I'm not going to cry
when a humorist in the CIA
appropriates this word.

In an etymological dictionary
I find the roots of his humour –
in Sanskrit slit and split.

Why should I cry when
I discover that 'rendition' his way
is the abstract noun used to hide the cries
of prisoners exported to be tortured?

'Song For Night'

Chris Abani's novella published by Akashic Books New York, 2007

(The officer in charge of the children is Major Essien according to his name tag.)

There will be no screams of pain
when landmines shatter these lives.

These boys and girls
are 'mine diffusers'

trained by 'John Wayne'
made to follow orders or die

their vocal cords cut
to ensure they cannot cry out.

There's nothing personal

Excuses from a board room

It's not that we don't care
but we've shareholders
to satisfy.

It's not that we don't care
but if we did it for you
all would expect it.

It's not that we don't care
but all this research
costs us money.

It's not that we don't care
but we're committed to
deregulation.

It's not that we don't care
but we need certainty
not uncertainty.

It's not that we don't care
but checking side effects
takes so much time.

It's not that we don't care
but our policy is choice
and freedom.

It's not that we don't care
but it's up to individuals
to make an effort.

If that means you lose
job, home and health
remember always
it's not personal.

To avoid thinking about the stock market

See tiny fruit begin to form
on apricot and plum.

Inhale the spring-time perfume
of glowing life in purple fig.

Pick a sweet Meyer lemon
to give zest to a casserole.

Enjoy white buds of Valencia
soon to bring orange blossom.

Take time to watch
mulberry leaves uncurl.

John Howard in Chicago

Mentor of the current Prime Minister

Excited, he's laughing
in this chaos, this cacophony
this golden cage for money-changers
this temple to capitalism
with a capital C.

'Elephants' trumpet and trample.
'Donkeys' bray in this zoo
where bulls bellow and
bears grunt to see which
will weigh in to win.

Buyers and sellers
shout the odds, watch the screens
gamble on futures –
in everything from armaments
to antiseptics.

There's ritual here
where the theories of
the Chicago School of Economics
and Milton Friedman
divide and rule.

Milton – that other Milton (John)
author of the *Areopagitica*
that seventeenth century tract
warned of 'the whole noise of
timorous and flocking birds.'

And Friedman –
irony in the sound of
'freedman' – chains us
to those speculative schemes
of dealers in this 'den of thieves'.

But that PM was comfortable, relaxed
flattered by being feted on the floor
of that Exchange, puffed up his chest
and to a question about our future
replied, 'I don't invest.'

Time to reflect on core promises

When is a core not a core?

When a servant of the people
denies the need to care
about the flesh that
keeps it whole.

Then it becomes the
harsh echoing caw of
a scavenging crow
flying low over
dying land.

Provoked by the Spring Racing Carnival *

Good afternoon ladies and gentlemen
they're just leaving the saddling paddock
ready to make their way to the starting gates
for the beginning of this year's special race –
the 2005 Senate Handicap.

It's perfect weather – not a cloud in the sky –
ASIO is first on to the track. He's in the box seat
carrying the lightest weight.

Shoot-to-Kill, a toey young two year old
is being ridden by an apprentice jockey who
we fear might not be strong enough
to stop him from bolting.

Sedition, an aged solid grey gelding
has a jockey on board who has been
up before the stewards on many occasions
for his bustling tactics that have caused
more than one horse and rider to fall –
he wears the colours of the Attorney General.

Pre-emptive Detention – sorry ladies and gentlemen –
Preventive Detention carries the hopes of his
foreign owners who have brought him
'down under' to win this race.

There's Habeas Corpus looking his usual self
but he's been drawn so wide his trainer fears
he'll have difficulty making up ground.

We've just been notified – ladies and gentlemen –
that the stewards have asked the owners of
Judicial Independence to explain why
she's been scratched at this late stage.

Now here comes the horse we've been waiting for.
Howard's Revenge is prancing, tossing his head,
perfectly prepared. He appears to see himself
the winner even before the race has begun.

* In July 2005 at the Federal election, John Howard gained control of the Senate

Thinking of the Garden of Australian Dreams in the National Museum

Sitting here at the kitchen table
I'm wondering if that guide
with his smooth bald head and
clipped un-Australian accent
might have been right.

This landscape of concrete
rise and fall is meant to
unite past and present
while we walk over
its multiple maps.

Surveyors' marks – poles
of red and white – superimpose
English names over names of
Aboriginal language groups,
mark pride in oil cattle uranium.

Memories of Shrapnel Valley
buttress the sides of a black tunnel
lit by low blue lights where
children's echoing voices know
nothing of this homage to mining.

A stand of slender trunks of
spindly gums – delicate, fragile –
opposes the rich dark green of
exotic Italian elms that mark
the edge of a pathway.

I look for other signs of
our history – there's Roxby Downs
but not Maralinga – and the
Never Never Graves leave out
the 'nigger hunts' in Mrs Gunn's book.

Quirky Aussie humour –
we are told – is there in
blue-painted telegraph poles
while shades of Nolan's 'Ned Kelly'
appear in the Camera Obscura.

Does that same humour invest
a black figure high up outside
the white windowless square –
with feet back to front – a mediaeval
idea of an Antipodean 'Down Under'?

So white that blank wall
pure white – not a fleck of
any other colour on
this house of Australian dreams
in this land with its red earth.

We are invited to lie on
a blue leather mattress inside
that hard-edged framed white space
shutting out what we don't want to see
where we can only stare at the sky.

Outside a separate place where
Aboriginal Australia has been given
space to share its millennia of stories
the great horizontal trunk of an ancient
eucalypt lies reflected in water.

At home, thinking about that visit
I realise, in the cold barren landscape
of that Garden of Australian Dreams
those White Australian Dreams
there was no place for women.

'That Stuff's Past'

Thinking of Dawn Casey, the first Curator of the National Museum

and

John Howard's response to an author wanting to collect the speeches of political leaders to examine changing approaches to Australian identity

Who chose that woman?
Who made her curator of
our Commonwealth Museum?

Who gave her the right
to give all that open space to
her fifty thousand years?

Who let her take space that
could have been given to what
we've done in our two hundred years?

How dared she believe
she had the right to rearrange
the significance of timelines in that way.

Well, now she knows.
Her contract was not renewed.
We will have no more of that!

Watching the Walkleys on SBS

It's luck again
using the remote
to find something
to keep me here
away from bed.

I stumble on it
just as Anton of
the golden voice
calls this stranger
to the stage.

He comes out
grabs each side
of the lectern
thrusts out his
pugnacious chin.

His voice is
rough demanding
'Men and women
of Australia' –
I'm with him.

Leaning forward
I await the order
'Come with me.
We're near Kirribilli.
Storm the barricades.

Let's get the
lying little rodent
and throw him
in the harbour.'
We cheer, we clap.

I almost stand –
he and we who
applaud have just
been guilty of an
act of sedition.

I go to bed happy.

A Small Matter

After seeing the Iranian film A Separation

The faceless judge dismisses them.
Theirs is a small matter – they waste his time.
Go home, sort out this problem of the visa.
You have forty days before it expires.

The wife wants the three of them,
husband, daughter and herself to leave
but he cannot, will not leave his father
and their daughter intends to stay.

Suffering from dementia, the old man
cannot be left alone. She argues
'He does not know you, your father's gone.'
Angry, she leaves, goes home to mother.

The carer she finds has her problems.
She must ring her Imam, ask a question.
Will she soil her soul if she touches him
and wipes the genitals of a stranger?

I sit there in that dark place far from
their agony of choices. He needs to work
and protect his father. The wife needs to escape
Visas are so rare. Time is racing past.

The husband of the carer, unemployed,
in debt, imprisoned by creditors, shamed
does not know his wife is working, hears
she has miscarried – the baby was a son.

Accused of pushing her down stairs
the husband is taken to court – and here
there is hope. If he admits the charge and
pays the victim, her husband can pay his debt.

It is a small matter. She only need swear
it happened. Does he want to die, leave his
daughter, his father? Better admit the crime,
better to pay, come to an agreement and pay.

But if she swears on the Qu'ran he caused
the death of her baby she will soil her soul
and she will not lay her hand on that Book
even if the husband she loves is dishonoured.

How many more small matters come before
faceless judges holding the power of life
or death in this land where the law –
theocratic and inflexible – is merciless?

Provoked by an item in the *Weekend Australian* 5–6 August 2006

'Cardinal Pell says he wants the church in Redfern to move away from social work and concentrate on souls.'

He's brought in Spanish missionaries
told them to take over the place
once the home, a spiritual home
where black voices filled the nave
sang with love, shared with love
knew, all the time, they were loved.

He's brought in Spanish missionaries
told them to bring with them
their Neo Cat-e-chu-men-al Way,
a way, a new conservative way,
such a long way from the path
Father Ted Kennedy trod.

Brought in pell-mell from Spain,
these priests who prefer to break
secret bread baked to some strict recipe
with Redfern's comfortable middle class
will not touch bread meant to feed fifty –
would not soil their hands to feed five thousand.

They've been told they're not there
for the body – only for the invisible soul.
And they've come from Spain where
separation of soul from tempting flesh
meant bodies were set on fire in autos da fé –
but I'm not to think of Torquemada today.

I must not remember Spain – Franco's Spain –
backed by the old conservative Catholic way
willing to torture, preferring dictatorship to
an elected government that just might take
some of their hierarchical privileges away.
No! I mustn't see those ways here today.

Today I stare at a photograph of daring work
by Aborigines painted on the Church wall
with words of an old conservative Pole,
words of the previous Pope – John Paul
telling the sacred truth he found in the way
of the Kamilaroi people of this land.

His black face is lined, his eyes show the pain.
This artist has brought this truth back again
to the church emptied of compassion and care
he's brought together those Papal words with
the totems of his people – emu and goanna –
the life Father Kennedy lived with his friends.

And what does the Neo Cat-e-chu-men-al Way
offer to those who knew Ted Kennedy's care?
In obscurantist language, hiding emptiness in
Middle English, French, Latin and Greek it offers
the elitism that sounds like Opus Dei – and
'Love thy neighbour as thyself' has no place there.

Conversation at Lucia's

Remembering Descartes' dictum 'je pense donc je suis' or 'Cogito ergo sum' ('I think therefore I am.')

Here, where aromas, perfumes test and tempt the senses
where shoppers come with wheeled wire baskets, walking
    frames
walking sticks, back packs, eco-friendly bags and children
in prams, on thighs, in arms, on shoulders, piggy-backed
or held by the hand – happy, contented, tearful or tired –
here, where we sip coffee and chat, he makes it clear.

Here, I feel it – feel that touchstone on the pulse –
know I must attack that so convenient separation
of mind from flesh, head from hand, intellect from
senses, ideas from consequences, so convenient
now for the more than three hundred long years
that men – well mainly men – have played that game.

He reminds me when he speaks of Jaime Guzman
Professor of Law at the Catholic University of Chile,
proud of his support for Pinochet – Franco's protegé –
proud it was his mind, his conception that laid down
the structure, the intellectual framework for this
secretive, cruel US-backed, ruthless regime.

So proud, in his safe intellectual tower, he
felt none of the pain, had no electrodes put
to his testicles, smelt none of the faeces,
heard none of the moans and screams of
those reduced by rape, saw none of the blood
tasted none of the grief in mothers' tears.

Jaime Guzman was proud – doing God's work –
raised by his intellect above the common herd
protected by that separation – his mind free
to act with impunity – he had no need to
feel what his laws might mean for those
who cried for mercy on the ground.

It's called the Cartesian principle –
that proof of who I am is in the power
of thought alone – safe from the
senses, feelings, hopes, fears and
consequences – and it has protected
Descartes' disciples for far too long.

James Wolfensohn on the *7.30 Report*

I see him on the screen
quiet, contained, strong white hair
plentiful across that round head
crowning that round face
matching that round
cuddly grandfatherly
shape.

I see him sitting there
cheerful, comfortable, benevolent
bringing to mind those chubby
fatherly Dickensian figures
whose role it was to ease
the burdens of the
abused.

I hear his carefully-measured
quietly-spoken words giving us those
numbers – one thousand billion dollars –
one thousand billion dollars –
money spent each year
on armaments and
war.

He's telling all of us
the world is out of balance –
one thousand billion dollars for
war and Son of Star Wars
but only fifty billion
to meet human
needs.

A banker – in fact –
President of the World Bank
that once forced dirt-poor countries
into cash crops sold for pittances
to multi-national companies,
he shows us this
imbalance.

And the poor, he says
treble in numbers as he speaks –
for them so little, for war so much
and, in that urbane tone he
almost seems to whisper
poverty promotes
terror.

Cluster bombs again – in August 2011

Israel dropped 1,200,000 cluster bombs, bought from USA, on Southern Lebanon in the three days before the cease-fire was signed. And five years on from 2006, Australia still refused to rule out their use so it could play its war games with the USA which still uses them in Afghanistan.

Five years on with almond trees now in bloom
our Minister for Defence defends the indefensible.

Then I saw clusters of white blooms of Satsuma plum
crowding branches offering themselves to bees.

Bunches of long-lasting lilac wallflowers
perfumed the air on tips of sun-seeking stalks.

Translucent tepals of soft scarlet begonias
glowed in Adelaide's dry cold morning light.

Clusters of cream Mahogany gum blossom
gave lorikeets a place to feed and play.

Buds of Valencia clustering between leaves
promised fragrant orange blossom and fruit.

Round heads – multiple flowers of orchid
offered their orange-gold brilliance to the sun.

Even today, whenever these clusters drop to earth
not one will kill a weary mother or unwary child.

Yet five years on we still lack courage, refuse to outlaw
these weapons because we want to play war games with
USA.

Constructing a hell on earth

Israel's actions in Gaza and the West Bank described on '360 Documentaries' Radio National 9 September 2012 and brought up to date

We will let you know we are here
invade your homes at night
divide men from women
let you have one room –
if we decide to stay
drive you out.

We will let you know we are here
terrify you with constant attacks
burning you all, young and old
bomb with white phosphorus
reduce your homes to rubble
deny you the right to work.

We will let you know we are here
we plan to break your heart and will
throw stones down your wells
use Ottoman laws to take land
force you to leave it fallow
so we can make it ours.

And we will build a hell on earth with hatred
either side of that great concrete wall
so no one will sleep easy at night
and homes reduced to rubble
will remind all who survive
of the price of bigotry while
hatred kills more children.

Was this satire too subtle?

After watching a performance of Adolf *written and performed by Pip Utton of the Centre for International Theatre as part of the Adelaide Fringe Festival 2011*

And after seeing the Nazi salute given by a member of the new Australian Defence League in a photograph in the Herald Sun

I could feel the relief – we all did.
He could take off the mask
get rid of the slicked down black wig
plastered diagonally across his brow
take off the tell-tale moustache
remove that brown shirt and
crooked cross arm band
loosen the tie, unbutton
that top button and
become one of us.

He could leave behind him
those last words *he* spoke
to the German 'Volk'
justifying his acts
punctuating them
by punching fist
again and again
into his palm.

And we could share that feeling –
after all this was no longer our world.
We had moved on, as he so
clearly was seeking to do –
this ordinary bloke
relaxing on stage.

He shared our hopes and fears.
We just want to protect our land,
our families, our children,
our language, our culture
didn't we?

That's what we had fought for
wasn't it? That's why our heroes died
hadn't they? He had us nodding as
he chatted and gazed out to us
sitting there in the dark,
listening, smiling
agreeing.

And we wanted to honour our heroes
didn't we? We could honour them
here and now, not with cheers,
but with a salute like this and
half that audience did.

A few turned, seeking agreement
uncertain, troubled, unsure.
A couple left the theatre but
I stayed there in the dark
waiting, fearful, tense
as he smoothed us
soothed us.

For so many he seemed just a bloke
a thoughtful bloke – one of us –
saying what so many felt
until, in that last minute,
when, beguiling and
asking to be let in
he clenched a fist
banging it hard
into the palm
of his hand.

History through the Centre for International Theatre

After watching Guy Masterson bring us Shylock through Tubal in Garth Armstrong's one man play Shylock

Through Shylock's only friend
he brings us the blindness of fanatics –
For Puritans, theatre contaminates.

In the 17th century Cromwell proclaims –
no audience will be tainted, no soul soiled
by a single word, phrase or gesture.

In the 18th century a woman – Bowdler's sister –
preserves the niceties, no vulgar suggestion
no Falstaffian quip will assail genteel ears.

In the 19th century Germans are entranced by
Shakespeare's *Merchant of Venice* with Shylock
played by a Romanian Jew until 1933.

But *The Merchant of Venice* is special.
This, Hitler's favourite play, must be adapted
purified to comply with his racial creed.

Shylock's daughter must not be Leah's child.
With a Christian mother, from a fling with the Jew
she will not bear the disgrace of that matriarchal line.

Lorenzo is safe. With Jessica and her father's gold
no Jewish ovaries will greet his Christian sperm
no Hebrew blood stain the pure Aryan line.

Now, in this 21st century listening to Andreas Scholl,
soaring with the ethereal voice of this German counter-
  tenor
I learn his harpsichord partner in life was born in Israel.

Not just another acronym

There's that ugly four-letter *just*
just a housewife, *just* a teacher
just a mother and now
just another acronym.

But this time it could have been
J. C. Williamson and memories
of Adelaide's Theatre Royal,
the view from 'the gods',
Roy Rene, sorrow in laughter,
music and Gladys Moncrieff
holding herself upright
at the foot of those stairs
refusing to let age defeat
'our Australian Glad'.

JCW – an acronym on an e-mail –
an irritant, just another code to be
deciphered opening only to
the electronically initiated.

That JCW and *The Maid of the Mountains*
fade as the message becomes clear.
These are women, sisters, mothers
Israeli mothers sharing the agony
of their Palestinian sisters,
wanting to find a way
without killing.

This is the
Jerusalem Centre for Women.

The price we pay for blindness

Following the interview of Professor Brian Holden by Richard Aedy in Sunday Profile *on ABC Radio National, 11 May 2014*

Today I discover we have a government
blind to the value of collaboration
indifferent to the role of sight in
learning for all these children.

It prefers its blinkered, self-centred view
there in the businessmen it chose to
decide who would go without
who would be denied hope.

Safe behind the wall of their wealth
they have decided we do not need
a Cooperative Research Centre
to encourage collaboration.

Once upon a time we had a government
believing in collaborative research
encouraging advances through
investing in our initiatives.

That is how Professor Brian Holden
began his work to give sight to
millions of girls and boys
suffering from myopia.

They needed the diagnosis by those
trained to do the work in villages
where the poor could not pay
where glasses cost so much.

With their help he was able to build Vision Centres
in countries around the globe where
children could not learn because
their eyesight was too poor.

Private-public partnership was made possible
and these CRCs set up in 1990 provided
avenues for science and industry to
advance private and public good.

These CRCs have brought profit to the nation as
well as the partners who chose cooperation
but this government's Commission of Audit
prefers to be blind and we have no one –
no King Lear to remind us about the
price a nation pays for blindness.

After that election

Acknowledging Sister Janet Mead

I see her standing
on the lowest stair.

Behind her, smiling
Don Quixote's Dulcinea

freed from that prison
of contempt and cruelty.

On stage performers
freed from their prison

of despair, thrilled
by their achievement.

I see her standing
in the spotlight

grey-haired, slight,
waiting, still –

waiting for ringing
cheers to subside.

She tells us why
they chose this play.

Her voice, so quiet
is heard by all.

We are in prison –
its bars the preference

for greed and mediocrity.
Tears begin to fall.

In this school hall
she offers hope.

In this school hall
I feed on her strength.

Voltaire's *Candide* by Mark Ravenhill at the Swan Theatre, Stratford-upon-Avon

A satire on optimism and the Panglossian doctrine brought frighteningly up-to-date becomes even more frightening when I return home

Am I in the best of all possible worlds
with this Prime Minister speaking of
optimism while he describes as 'freed'
all those workers sacked in industries?

Am I in the best of all possible worlds
when this Prime Minister begins to
get rid of this nation's greatest gift
to its people, universal health care?

Am I in the best of all possible worlds
with a Prime Minister happy for States
to cut the water supply to Aboriginal land
and force families to leave their homes?

Am I in the best of all possible worlds
with a Prime Minister eager to be punitive –
funding truancy officers while removing
aid for Aboriginal students through ITAS?*

Am I in the best of all possible worlds
with a Prime Minister who puts down
so much to 'the lottery of life', and adds
to the burdens of the poorest of women?

Am I in the best of all possible worlds
when this Prime Minister reduces refugees
to refuse to be dumped out of sight and mind
by officials he requires to be callous?

Am I in the best of all possible worlds
when this Prime Minister decides to put
the despot who made life intolerable for
refugees in charge of our social security?

Am I in the best of all possible worlds
when this Prime Minister withdraws funds
from charitable not-for-profit groups since
in his view compassion is 'moral vanity'.

Am I in the best of all possible worlds
with a Prime Minister cutting tape,
red and green, for all those magnates
turning our land into a gigantic quarry?

Am I in the best of all possible worlds
with a Prime Minister who speaks of
optimism while making the young and
older pay so much more for education?

Am I in the best of all possible worlds
while his Foreign Minister, lying in Lima,
denies our Great Barrier Reef is in danger
seeing no problem with all this dredging?

Am I in the best of all possible worlds
when his Minister for the Environment
tries, at his command, to remove from
the World Heritage List our ancient forests?

Am I in the best of all possible worlds
with a Prime Minister unwilling to fund
a scientific future for all of us that might
offer us hope for a self-reliant nation?

Am I in the best of all possible worlds
when we have a Prime Minister intending
to use fear and patriotism and his media to
blind all to what his budget will cost us?

Am I in the best of all possible worlds
when a Prime Minister, resenting criticism,
forces our ABC to destroy regional services
when he swore to us 'No cuts to the ABC.'?

Can I possibly be in the best of all possible worlds
with a Christian Prime Minister before Christmas
crippling the work of generous advocates fighting
for those who are blind, deaf, disabled or homeless?

How long must I survive in this world of his?
While fifty two percent of us are quite content
and, feeling they are safe, say to the rest of us
'So long as I'm all right, Jack, you can go to hell!'

*ITAS, the Indigenous Tutorial Assistance Scheme, has been supporting Aboriginal and Islander students in primary, secondary and tertiary institutions, enabling them to succeed in the mainstream of the Australian system of schooling. As of 16/9/14 it was expected to be cut. $28 million was put into truancy officers. In total $534 million was removed from Indigenous support services.

The United Nations International Day for the Abolition of Slavery December 2nd 2011

'Amazing Grace'

Black Americans brought this hymn into their gospel music
singing it as they prayed for equality in their Civil Rights campaign.

This hymn came, in its American guise, via the Second Great Awakening
and found its way into *Uncle Tom's Cabin* by Harriet Beecher Stowe.

In the depths of his great crisis Uncle Tom sang three of its verses,
two by its English author, one from an old sacred ballad sung by slaves.

Her story fired the hearts of America's fighters against slavery
and played a part in the events leading to that ferocious Civil War.

This hymn, from England, was written by a once sea-going reprobate –
press-ganged, a deserter, later slave trader, led through storm to faith.

Ordained, a curate serving in Olney, by then preaching against that trade
with a fellow evangelist, the poet William Cowper, he wrote hymns.

Believing now that only God's amazing grace had saved his soul
he composed this hymn in 1773 for a sermon to be given on New Year's Day.

Seven years later, their Olney hymns in print, a minister in a London parish
John Newton was heard by a Member of Parliament, William Wilberforce.

Among the philanthropic causes he took up was the abolition of
the slave trade and he did not give up until it was abolished in 1807.

Slavery was officially abolished in the British empire in 1833. During
the American Civil War a new gun, the Gatling gun, mowed down hundreds.

Mahalia Jackson, with that history alive in her, says singing this hymn
gives 'the joy felt at being delivered from slavery and worldly miseries.'

The editor of an anti-slavery anthology believes it has the power 'to turn
alienation into empathy ... the unspeakable into imaginative literature.'

WE GAVE
POWER
TO THOSE WITH STONES
WHERE THEIR
HEARTS
MIGHT BE

At an Australian Suburban Swimming Pool

The child is here again
leading his mother by the hand,
eager to join friends, water babies,
paddling in the pool.

Beneath that young crop
of soft light auburn curls
secure, he surveys his world,
wide brown eyes alert.

Behind those smiling eyes
no need for watchfulness.
Nodding at instructors he makes
his small purpose plain.

In time, he will move up
become a 'tadpole', then a 'seahorse'
torn by no nightmare of pain and fear
no memory of prison wire.

His mother has never had to
hold him tight in a boat at sea
hoping they will reach harbour
to be given kindly asylum.

He need never feel her terror
of what tomorrow might bring.
He'll not be woken at three am
to be forced to leave a refuge.

He is a winner in this gamble,
in what this Prime Minister can
shrug off as 'the lottery of life'
with its see-saw of win or lose.

This boy's mother need not
risk her life, fearing tomorrow's
suicide bomber's random act
or the next day's fanatical rage.

She need not prepare herself
for that next act of indifference
in the name of 'Stopping the Boats'
so her child must live with her fear.

Here, this child is free not to know.
He can remain innocent for a while.
Safe, inside these 'sovereign borders'
he is free to kick his legs and swim.

Is this Reconciliation?

He had made that speech
had made it so well that
he gave them hope.

He had said 'Sorry',
promised respect
support and honour.

We felt we had made
our confession and
received absolution.

So now we could deny
requests to show respect
to their sacred monolith

make noises of concern
at preventable diseases
swear to bridge the gap

while we refused houses
until traditional owners
leased their land to us.

We could dismiss those
who dared to leave towns
escaping grog and pain

remain deaf to doctors who
insisted their health is better
on those homelands

those places a Minister
jeered at and rejected as
just 'cultural museums'.

Seven years on and still
subject to 'Interventions'
they are kept dependent.

Our money pays truancy officers
sees the stick as the way to make
parents send children to school

So Rosalie Kunoth-Monks
whose home is in Utopia,
shown in that film to those
willing to open their eyes,
tells all watching this Q & A
'I am a cultural woman
I am not the problem.'

New installation in the South Australian Museum

They stand in the corner
just outside the entry
to the Aboriginal Gallery.

Cylindrical, slightly inclined
thick, tall, thin, small
men women children

made from the inner bark
of Kurrajong, earth pigments
beeswax, feathers, string

some marked with red ochre
others yellow for those
of different families

while, for those unknown
the heads of their burial poles
have been left bare.

These poles speak for the dead
so many shot – 'bang bang'
in those killing times

when pastoralists tried to
and often did wipe out
whole generations

of the Yolgnu people
at Florida Station but
could not kill all.

For Our Forefathers
brought into being
by *Ten Canoes*

belongs in Australia's
traditional history and
should be compulsory.

Three portraits by Julie Dowling

Included in the exhibition in the Flinders City Gallery celebrating 21 years of the Yunggorendi First Nation Centre through the collection of the work of Aboriginal artists in 'Long Way Home', Tracey Bunda describes the portraits in the commentary that accompanies them

Each portrait glows.
Soft dark faces
youthful cheeks
warm quiet eyes
thoughtful, alert
three young men
Aboriginal men.

Did Rembrandt teach her
show her how to bring
the soul to the surface
through subtle textures
of light and shade?
Did he provide for her
this way to make us see?

Presented here with
their youthful beauty
who, in the name of
free speech, believes
he has the right not to
respect their humanity
to jeer in terms of abuse
to deny them the dignity
of their family names?

String Games – thinking of Kaurna Elder Dr Lewis O'Brien

On a work of art in the foyer of the addition to South Australia's State Library

I

I look up at that
double-looped, heavy
disembodied clumsy
make-believe meant
to bring to mind
string games.

It's meant to honour
fibre culture – but that
ever still horizontal
double loop will never
come sliding from
an old man's pocket.

We must look up
discover in the shape
the living meaning
of it all. This fibre rope
will never curl around
old dextrous fingers.

But I have seen him
on a kindergarten chair
stooping towards faces
raised from the floor,
chins cupped in hands
insisting on respect.

He will not teach –
he will not weave
stories of their past
with quick-silver
fingers making
new games.

He waits and waits,
this Kaurna Elder,
unwilling to go on
and share his skill
until their hearts
are in his hands.

I look up again
at this work hanging
in mid-air above
a binary carpet
that looks to
an abstract future.

And I want
on these flat white
hard, cutting-edged
angular twenty-first
century walls
hands.

I want hands, faces,
eyes gleaming
in anticipation
the young learning
with string and fingers
intertwining.

II

He's here, sees me, smiles –
the ironic 'Isle of Refuge' exhibition
has brought us together again.

What does he think of
that thing hanging there
lifeless, disembodied?

'They want to honour us –
this is their way –
it's theoretical.'

'But you have never
been disconnected
from the earth.'

He smiles.

Two Aboriginal Women

Acknowledging Lillian Holt and Lowitja O'Donoghue at a WomenSpeak Conference

One named Lillian
stands on that stage,
bright in vivid green
laughing, telling jokes
breaking down walls
between women who
now want to learn
instead of preach. She
leaves us with a phrase
that silences laughter
reminding us racism is
the gangrene of the soul.

Grey-haired, stalwart
Lowitja has fought
so long with dignity
refusing to let those
drive-by shooters
kill her spirit. She
calls up so many
women to that stage
black beside white
holding hands eager
to learn the words of this
new song for an old land
'The Journey of Healing'.

After looking at the paintings of Desert Country by the Warakurna Artists Desert Mob and taking home the record of their work

Desert Country *by Nici Cumpston with Barry Patton*
Art Gallery of South Australia, Adelaide

My fingers feel the texture
trace each letter in the title
there and not there with
its absence of colour
beneath the richness of
'Ngayuku ngara –
My country' painted in
red ochres and black
mapping from the sky
tracks and places
of their land.

Those records of country
rest on my lap so I feel
their heaviness and
the weight of time
tracing places
and Dreamings
of Honey Ant
and Moon.

I read the dedication.
These artists share with all
who feel the power they hold
true stories of their land.
With a generous spirit
they offer this record
in friendship to all
who pause, read
and are willing
to go on to
that last
work.

Maralinga.

Radio National Breakfast, 26 August 2014

Frank Walker: Maralinga: Shame and betrayal in the Australian desert

When seven atomic bombs exploded
at Maralinga Britain had great hopes.

The results of that experiment might
help Britain to be a player in the game.

Scientists knew winds would carry fallout
south into the continent's coastal cities.

Scientists, certain they need not care
about ethics at all, examined the bones

babies' bones to be taken for twenty years
searching for evidence of strontium 90

recording the results (only for Britain)
of nuclear rain far from that desert site.

No one knew. Robert Menzies kept
quiet about the use of this 'empty land'

he gave to Britain's scientists
handing it over to them carte blanche.

The author calls it 'the great betrayal'
a betrayal of military men deployed there.

Awake in bed, avoiding winter's chill
I listen and hope and wait and wait.

Surely, surely, they will speak about it –
make mention of that greater betrayal

the betrayal of the owners of that land
their home for fifty thousand years.

But in 1957 these people had no rights –
they had no place in the Constitution.

That Prime Minister had no need to recognise
them. They were not even forgotten families

and could be shifted, moved wherever he liked.
Surely in 2014 they will be remembered.

Not so. All talk of political indifference to
compensation focuses only on the forces.

A deeper chill is finding its way into my bones.
Fifty years on their suffering can still be dismissed.

Indigenous culture in an interdisciplinary curriculum

Christopher Pyne dismisses the relevance of Australian or other Indigenous cultures as interdisciplinary connections with the sciences in Australia's national curriculum

Just as he sees no connection between mathematics and sustainability
he will not recognise the ingenuity, the understanding of
aerodynamics in the form of different boomerangs.

He will not recognise the depth of thought, the experiments
the decisions, the trial and error that produced these
most amazing tools providing food for families.

They are not instruments made of bronze, copper, iron.
Worked in wood with stone they do not count. Only
what's found in his western world matters to him.

He will not recognise the physics in these inventions
won't see craftsmanship or admire the ideas that
kept their culture alive for over 50,000 years.

And what of the woomera, increasing thrust and distance.
And what of bush medicine – the botany of their flora
that companies now seek to patent for profit.

And what of their pharmaceutical knowledge promoting healing –
kangaroo apple for swollen joints, Kakadu plum for Vitamin C?
Scientists now want to use emu bush to sterilise implants.

He'll have a place for Greek astronomers. They belong to the west.
But what of the sun as Walu, a woman, lighting her fire each day
and scattering red ochre across the clouds to create dawn?

If he can, he'll ensure none of our children experiences
the wonder in these ways, scientific ways, that helped
them thrive across this immense continent without
men and women in white coats in laboratories.

To a woman named Grace

A South Australian Minister for Aboriginal Affairs and Reconciliation in 2010

I have a friend named Grace
always kindly, always respectful
finding ways, small and generous
to lift the spirits of others.

She knows the sacred from the profane
and in all the forty years
since she came to my rescue
has brought laughter to my life.

I read the message of anger and grief
from the Adnyamanthanha people.
Another Grace, named for God's gift,
has just betrayed that name

so eager to please a Premier who brags
of increase in numbers, now twelve
great quarries tearing into the earth
for short-term gain scaring the land.

He made her Minister for Aboriginal Affairs
and Reconciliation – gave her charge
of this State's First Nations.
It looks good to have a woman in this role.

He knew there would be no respect
for them, their families, their memories,
the spiritual connection for millennia
that lives in and feeds their land.

These are not Christian or even Moslem burial sites.
These have no value to be measured in dollars
and, besides, we don't really need to care –
negotiation demands respect and time.

So, this graceless woman has made it law –
a mining company is to be allowed 'to damage,
disturb or interfere with any sites,
remove any object or remains in this area'.

They are 'remains' now, 'objects',
'remains' – as much animal as human –
'objects' – not artefacts to be dusted
gently touched by archaeologists with respect

only with permission from traditional owners.
This woman does not deserve her given name.
She has played her part – roughshod and ruthless
revealing the sham that is 'reconciliation'.

'Symbols are what Aboriginal people no longer need.'

An Editorial in the Australian *about Michael Long's Walk to talk to Australia's Prime Minister*

Thank you Mr Editor –
you simplify our world.

Is there any need for
the rising sun with
emu feathers on
an old slouched hat?

any need for cross and
crucifix, crescent
bread and wine
or holy grail?

any need for a wailing wall
wreaths at Lone Pine
poppy fields in Flanders
marking sites of grief?

or for lion and unicorn
France's chanticleer
that great bald eagle
or the Russian bear?

or for stars and stripes
red maple leaf on white
India's spinning wheel
Ireland's singing harp?

You tell them, Mr Editor –
you simplify their world.

They've no need of
black for their people
their golden sunlit disk or
red for their story-filled land.

Damn it all, I'm weeping again

After seeing Pecan Summer *again, the Indigenous opera written and directed by Deborah Cheetham*

He is angry, feels let down now.
It has been a bolt from the blue.
His good and great friend has
decided he dare not change
Section 18c of the Racial
Discrimination Act. For once
decency and respect have won.

He will not be able to take from
this fine pale-faced bass baritone
grandson of a Yorta Yorta Elder
his ancestry. He will not be able
to berate him because of his pale face
or deny this singer his inheritance
by insisting this must be a false identity
and he cannot be an Aborigine.

On stage with his voice bringing
to all of us the extraordinary courage of
his grandfather and his role in the story
we are brought close to their suffering
and their fear for young families.
We live the history in his song and
come to feel the love, lifted to
a new level of understanding.

We hear why his grandfather
dared to take his family and
walk away from Cummeragunja.
Starving on the mission with
their 'Protector' selling their food,
denied the right to meet together
without his permission, and with
women so frightened – they had to leave.

We must thank those descendants
no longer afraid, prepared to fight
to take to court this journalist
who would now keep them out
of Australia's Constitution, deny
their past *and* their right to belong.
In the theatre again, I clap and weep.
Their victory has not yet been overthrown.

A date we must remember: 4 July 2014

The day the real Tony Abbott stood up
and we saw him for who he is

It took one word followed by two more
'unsettled' or 'scarcely settled' to wipe out
fifty thousand years of occupation.

Fifty thousand years still here in
a living culture, its art, its petroglyphs
its cosmology linking earth and sky.

Fifty thousand years of human life
with trade routes, exchange of goods,
weapons, tools, implements designed.

Fifty thousand years of stories, moral tales
about the cost of greed and selfishness
denying families the food they need to share.

Fifty thousand years of teaching and learning
with men and boys, girls and women in
bora ring and art learning laws and language.

Fifty thousand years of stories in dance
dancing the land, honouring spirits in
rocks, rivers, trees in music and ceremony.

Fifty thousand years dismissed in his words
as though they had never been since 'settled'
for him can mean only the culture he values.

A darker matter

Thinking of Lal Bibi

Hidden under her burqa she is expected to carry the burden
be willing to kill herself, acknowledging her dishonour.
That way she will free her family from disgrace but
she was dishonoured, kidnapped at eighteen
tortured, raped, chained for five days
by Afghan police officers.

Her suicide is not to remind them of her suffering.
It is to put behind them the fact of their cowardice –
it is to free them, these men, restore to them
their sense of honour for generations
re-establish their male supremacy
at all times, whatever they do.

Land Mines: A Love Story

ABC Channel 2

Mairy is carrying her fourth child
pressing in her womb on that right leg
she lost trying to save the family cow.

Under her blue burqa, sitting in the dust
her voice cries to men passing on two legs
for mercy and money to feed her family.

She's learnt to beware – yellow parcels
from the skies could be bombs not food,
might kill or maim the sons she has borne.

Where she seeks help to ease the pain
of that crude metal leg rubbing the stump,
all who serve are women who limp.

There's love behind the camera that
lets Mairy and Shah, both flowers from
the same garden, tell their Afghan story.

A permissible form of coercion?

Philip Ruddock who served in a number of portfolios in the Howard government was heard to say that sleep deprivation is a permissible form of coercion

I'm not allowed to sleep –
cannot ease my bones
lie down, close my eyes
in the kindly dark
that allows me to
breathe in and out
and forget the day.

I'm not allowed to sleep –
turn on my side
find peace in the pillow
hold around my neck
sheet and blanket to
keep my shoulders
from the cold.

I'm not allowed to sleep –
kept awake for hours
red eyeballs bulging
head too heavy
on my neck
not allowed to nod
or drift away.

I'm not allowed to sleep –
must hear those voices
pounding on and on
day after sleepless day.
They tell me if I will sign
what they want me to say
I can sleep for a week.

Considering education as nourishment

The impact of changes to the bridging visas for asylum seekers who arrived after a certain date

There's to be nothing to feed the mind
no easing of their burden of memories.

There is to be no nourishment from now on
no chance to seek the light, our light, in school.

Education is forbidden. No daily meeting with
other minds and hearts of students and teachers.

And if they have been learning at school
in hijabs or casual clothes, they must leave.

Our schools, the bread of life for our children
are not to be here for those who braved storms.

There are to be no connections, no shared
moments of delight as understanding grows.

Whatever release from fear, uncertainty or
longing they might have felt will be gone.

And if in their hearts there is a need to help
a desire to share, working without a wage

that generous impulse is to have no outlet.
If they volunteer, are caught, they will suffer.

There is always the threat of return to detention.
They may walk our streets, not enter our world.

After seeing the film *Healing*

Funded by Film Victoria and our Australian Broadcasting Corporation

I so wish we could live this way
knowing who we are in our heart
able to endure the rest.

I have listened to those words four times now
as the Iranian offender speaks in Farsi
to the wounded wedge-tailed eagle.

Both are prisoners learning before release
but I had missed the key in the past tense
'Know who you *were in your heart*.'

In his reminder to the majestic suffering bird
of the strength he had, that's what eighteen
years in prison are teaching him.

That knowledge offers a way to 'endure the rest'
wherever we might happen to be imprisoned
to hold, keeping inside, who we once were.

In this film we face the contrasts between
creatures of nature and human predators
preying on the young and weak.

We see the wounded, grief-stricken, ashamed
serving their time, helped and hindered
both by themselves and others.

This film has come just when we are discouraged
made to believe never again will we be able to be
generous, share our lives with laughter, tears, joy.

For we chose to bring to power those indifferent to
beauty, truth, honour and justice in life and art.
We let them put us behind their invisible bars.

We gave power to those with stones where their hearts
might be and, numbed by the cruelty and indifference,
I fear we did not value who we once were when we
lived as human beings in a civilised community.

Considering Chinese culture in science and mathematics

Christopher Pyne sees no value in the interdisciplinary approach that makes connections between Asian cultures and separate subject domains

He has established a new Colombo Plan
one where our top students will travel
enter their universities often
without their language or
feeling for their culture
just for our profit.

He sees no need, if they study in China,
for students to feel admiration for all
those inventions that came often
along the Silk Road to change
life in Europe for everyone
in navigation, books, war.

Not just the compass, printing, gunpowder.
With the abacus and shadow clock they
might have recorded a solar eclipse
in 2137 BC or BCE as it is now.
The Chinese abacus transferred
fingers to beads on a frame.

And who needs to admire curiosity
and the capacity for adaptation
the way another nation finds
to use its natural vegetation –
bamboo to make rods for
counting before 400 BCE?

What else will he leave out to
increase our general level
of ignorance as well as
arrogance in the new
national curriculum
he will establish?

Contemplating banners displayed in front of the Art Gallery

This is the work of the Russian artistic collective AES+F that gained favour at the Venice Biennale

Four great banners hang between sandstone pillars
so very clean, no smudge, no smear – purest white
of faces and limbs and clothes – spotless, sterile.

Young women lie on couches, a young man lifts a weight
another raises her bow, ready to fire an arrow –
they seem the epitome of physical perfection.

And there are subservient women and men
black and yellow, fulfilling all demands of these clients
kneeling, assisting, massaging and waiting.

My stomach churns. What am I being offered here?
Is it the return to that Aryan dream turned nightmare –
that Anglo-Saxon world and 'white Australia'?

No explanation removes the fear. What am I being told?
I ask a young man. He googles the Art Gallery –
these banners derive from Petronius, an ancient poet.

His epic poem – the *Satyricon*. I listen in disbelief.
Only if I find time and go inside will I find answers
answers I hope will ease the fears that grip my mind.

I do make time, go inside to the first floor to face
a gigantic screen spread across a whole gallery wall
a screen filled with bodies and classical German music.

White bodies, assured, expecting obedient service.
receiving it from black men in silk Chinese tops,
massaged by delicate, immaculate Chinese girls.

All is in slow motion: sometimes as if in a ballet
every move sensual in this temple to the perfect body
this temple of health with every modern machine.

And I ask myself. 'Will the worm turn?'
For me this is no fantasy, no 'Feast of Trimalchio'
no detached exploration of sybaritic pleasure.

Peacocks might fill the screen, spread their brilliant fans
with their hundred Argus eyes of ancient myth and
    memory –
great macaws might fly across the screen and sky

but no exotic birds, no ancient traditional architecture –
Corinthian capitals, pantheon of Rome, intricate Arabic
or imperial Chinese can dissipate my fear.

White arrows fly, answered by African spears and arrows
of a Native American chief, his servant garb gone, and
blood stains the white sports shirt of a pale-faced boy.

The worm turns. Servants put off their servitude
take over the couches. Now white women and men
offer lobster, wine and fruit to African and Chinese men.

But, as the attendants in the gallery tell us it's time to go
I leave with the image of that ageing white woman
still imperious, now in glowing African colours and feel
the story is not over. I should come back again.

WE·THE·PEOPLE·SURGE·IN·THE·SOUND·THE·SINGING·IN·THE·RHYTHM

Lessons from my three gardeners

In appreciation of Dante, Klaus and Viktor

I hear you, my kindly Italian gardener,
whose name brings me *The Divine Comedy*
teasing and laughing at me again.

When will I learn that I must wait
have patience. Peaches, cherries
will not come at my command.

* * * *

Your strength stays with me
there in your commitment
to the quality in the task.

With that strength always
the surprise and delight in
our shared love of music.

* * * *

Each teacher offers gifts –
this time ideas in books
speaking of science and life

while keeping that balance
between order and chaos
my green sanctuary needs.

In Grade VII – 1945

The government of South Australia says it intends to re-establish weekly testing since our NAPLAN results seem to be not as high as other States

Mushroom clouds in photographs
of black and white cry victory

but nothing changes the routine –
Friday is always test day.

Can I spell the word etiolation?
Do I need to know what it means?

Did I do an experiment to show
I know how the process works?

Do I recognise silent letters
in pneumonia or knowledge?

How many words do I have wrong?
How many times must I correct them?

How good am I at long division?
Can I find the highest common factor?

Can I show I know the difference
between radius and diameter?

What if I fear punishment at home
if I fail to reach the level *they* want?

This is the world our government
wants to bring back to schools in 2013.

Once more there will be no music –
while art will just be colouring in.

And one word will never have a place
in that weekly test – imagination.

Thanking the late John Griffin for that article in the SAIT Journal

You have my thanks at least in part
for telling the tale of awful
inexorable daily grind

to those who will not, cannot see
the time required
and energy

to second guess a vacant mind
or give the help an anxious class
requires.

You have my thanks at least in part
for showing the need
to disappear.

But what you couldn't make them hear,
see or smell were doorways
into dimlit hell

so frightening in their echoing way
where cold cement and water
froze fingers

rinsed under dripping taps
whose raps on tinny troughs
ricocheted off walls

where some might hide,
fill grey space with stench
of shit and nicotine

stuff ceramic bowls with paper,
blood-soaked pads, crushed
cigarettes or chips

and, to while away the time, climb
over a dunny wall via plastic lid
leaving it locked behind.

For others a stinking sanctuary
where tears and muffled sobs
could have some privacy.

Had this too been part of your
daily grind?

John Griffin of Adelaide, 1935–2012, was a very fine teacher, poet and writer of radio plays often performed on the ABC.

On the *7.30 Report*, Friday, 24 January 2014, the Chief Scientist, Professor Ian Chubb, speaking of mathematics, says that he wants us all in the same tent

If he does, we must remove segregation of students into supposedly separate cultures of science and mathematics versus the arts and humanities as well as the unwillingness of STEM to make interdisciplinary connections

Don't I as one of those deemed
inappropriate for that elite
have the right to access
their language?

to algebra, that Arabic word,
giving me letters in place
of apples or oranges to
to solve problems

to know what binary means
and be aware of the way
two numbers – one and
nought – affect us all

to find in *Alice in Wonderland*
the work and words of that
lecturer in mathematics
Lewis Carroll.

to discover diagrams, diagonals
and the diameter of circles
draw them with ruler,
pencil or compass

to learn about and not to fear
equations, recognise that
an equilateral triangle
has equal angles.

to remember what those
factors were in HCF
or see how they
work in 2 x 4 = 8?

And in geometry, do more
than recite off by heart
about the square on the
hypotenuse etcetera

think of a hemisphere as
a shape, not just us here
below the equator with
them on the other side.

Find in an inch more than
that awful saying 'Give
them an inch and they
will take a mile.'

Remember nothing that
speaks of 'j' except
it was no jolly fun
to be in that room

'k' bringing me the change from
chains, furlongs, fathoms to
kilometres, kilolitres, kilos
on weight loss programs.

And what was the length of
a piece of string? The long
and short of it all in a
parallelogram.

Man must measure – that book
a reminder of all the ways
we use measurement of
height, depth, width

but no maths teacher took me
to names, to people, – all
was number except one,
Pythagoras.

I should have liked mapping
seeing how maps changed
as explorers navigated
around the globe

that would have been a way
to open the mind to new
possibilities, feeling the
presence of people

but the entry of humanity
would undermine the
the numbers, letters
serving this God.

Mendel would have value in
botany and genetics but
would he have a place
in mathematics?.

Not wanting now to be obtuse,
insensitive or irritating I offer
this quick aside to all who
like me want to learn:

decades on I'd meet, work with
and come to love a Principal,
a mathematician, making
lemonade from lemons

from him I'd learn the minus sign
need not mean failure as it does
now in the numeracy tests
we put children through

those percentages always in reports
defining us – not ideas in words
bringing parabolas, polygons
perimeters to mind.

What right did they have to decide
we should be despised, thought
soft because we dared to think
of people before pie charts?

How often have the righteous destroyed
lives, denying access, giving no
quarter to those slower at
working out quotients?

At school I enjoyed right angles.
They gave me trigonometry
and before she focused us
on numbers – pyramids

for a minute, but not for long
I could delight in the way
a new connection was
being made for me.

What was the ratio of delight
to distress? I will not try to
calculate it now. Feelings
had no place there.

The speed of sound would matter
when a plane broke that barrier
and the speed of light would
take me later into space.

Square root signs I see them now.
I knew addition, subtraction,
multiplication, division but
had no time for statistics

statistics – those substitutes for people
that Principal valued, with those
mathematicians, Germain and
Gauss named for classrooms.

I grew to love him. People came first
in his school. Homesteads connected
to people – Blainey, Wright, Fulton,
Tjilbruke and Oliphant

so students knew people were there
always in the subjects they loved
or endured – or they had the
chance to realise that truth.

Tangents proffered possibilities
when I taught those boys who
set out to distract me
from my goal

offering new ways to cross that
man-made divide, take on
ideas that just might
make more sense

might bring unity, not division,
connections between number
and metre, ten syllables in a
line of poetry or perhaps

painters in their perspective,
might take the eye into the
landscape or vision to
that vanishing point.

Why did mathematicians
always seem to be men
when I knew women
teaching via plants

taking children out to study
weeds on a hillside to
measure their impact
on a bushland site

and another showing boys
the intricacy of number
in tap-dancing, playing
bridge for probability?

Why do men still leave women out
concentrating on abstractions
to ensure there is no room
for them in their realm?

Why did we have to wait for a woman
Margaret Wertheim, the author
of *Pythagoras' Trousers*, to
remind us of their work?

Why is it that it has taken a woman
to connect, for people eager to learn,
the joy she finds in literature and
her love of mathematics?

How many years must it take
before we reach the zenith
be allowed to feel the
connections that will
let us grasp the value
in the language of
mathematics?

Not if he can help it

Christopher Pyne sees no connection between Asian cultures, Indigenous cultures, sustainability, science and mathematics

The westward move of mathematics
through the Hindu-Arabic cultures
has no place in the mind of one
focused on western civilisation.

He does not care how zero entered the game –
the fact that it is there is enough because
it might be the difference between
being in or out after an election.

Why should he, so certain he knows everything
permit others – since he has the power –
to take in the work in mathematics
of men like Brahmagupta

or even earlier, Pingala, so long before Christ,
using binary numbers as short and long
syllables, making them similar to, but
long before, the Morse Code?

Aryabhata – of AD 498 – will have no place
although astronomy is the oldest
numerical science crucial for
calendars and navigation.

Aryabhata worked out what we now know
to be the origin of what we accept as
the 'modern, decimal-based place
value notation'.

There will be no exploration of minds
east of the Tigris and Euphrates.
Not if he can help it.

We have come so far from my childhood

Considering this children's book SCIENCE – The ultimate guide to the Scientific World

We've come so far from my childhood
from *Shoes, and ships and sealing wax*
from *Living things for lively youngsters*
and *More living things for lively youngsters*
with those pictures in black and white –
sketches that spoke of children drawing
and nothing in a spiral binding.

We've come so far from my childhood
and Australian stories of gumnut babies
and banksia men and stories too of 'home'
of ancient oaks, of willows and the piper
at the gates of dawn bringing a child
from 'down under' to listen to those tales
of a mole, a rat, a badger and a toad.

In that childhood I drew close
to living things – rich orange fungi
growing out of damp decaying wood,
that tough small plant growing beside
paths in the hills and bearing my name,
cockles, limpets and the occasional
jellyfish left behind as the tide went out.

Today, as I browse through bookshops
for books for the children of friends
I find another world, a world where
photons come into play on an image
a blue-eyed holograph such a long way
from the living science I explored and
I wonder what the future holds for them.

Considering reductionism in this new interpretation of the word 'kindle'

Acknowledging and quoting from The Math Book: From Pythagoras to the 57th dimension. 250 Milestones in the History of Mathematics *by Clifford A Pickover, published by Sterling Publishing Co. 2009*

That principal says students now have e-books.
No one needs all those printed pages.
Thousands of books, all shapes
colours, fonts, styles, sizes
offering life and nature are
there on their kindles
reduced – six by four –
available at a price
able to be moved
at a click up or
down with the
battery for a
percentage
to say how
far there is
to go.

This book, kindling its inspiring tales of mathematics
over aeons of time, will not make sense
that way, has dates vertically on the
left hand margin next to the words
and facing each story a picture of
the stage the story has reached.
First the ant odometer over
150,000,000 years ago
then cicada-generated
prime numbers before
homo sapiens began
with knots, found
in that *Book of*
Kells, offered
ideas to help
us unravel
the loop
of DNA!

But she, and all who follow her lead, without imagination,
dismiss the role of wonder.

Remembering the lost boys

In 2010 in South Australia the Enterprise Bargain with the AEU did not include teacher librarians as a essential part of the cohort of staff for a school
Dedicated to the late Doris Hunter of Mawson High School

They came for protection, those lost boys
knowing they would not be failed or judged
finding someone willing to help them read
where they need not hide behind that mask,
that tough mask of careless indifference.

They came to a person who would be firm
meet their needs, even take them further
so often beyond their wildest dreams
into worlds between pages where slowly
more confidently they made discoveries.

Some came at first for refuge from bullies
safe in the warmth, no-nonsense warmth
of that connection where no words in red
made them believe they were failures
where no one would jeer at their results.

Then they came to browse to take their time
follow up interests not wanted in classrooms
find in magazines ideas they might explore
taking them back to workshops to make them live
as forms, images, in metal, wood or clay.

But this State government decided our boys –
and girls – did not need the teacher librarians who
offer the broader vision subject teachers might lack.
This cost-cutting government preferred machines
to isolate the young hunched before the screens.

What indifferent bureaucrat gave that advice –
told thoughtless politicians interested primarily
in motor races, connecting an oval to a casino,
law 'n order and credit ratings that computers
would save government the cost of salaries?

Inert blank screens must be turned on to open,
shake no hands, cannot anticipate human needs
cannot express sympathy or delight when
a boy or girl comes in to share a success
and hear the pleasure in her words of praise.

Questions for the author of *Jane Austen is Dead*

Do you want to belong with
fanatics who deface ancient art
like the great Bamiyan statues?
Are you, too, an iconoclast?

What is it that you fear –
the revelation of character
the courage it always takes
to look beyond money?

Is it the quality of language
the delicate touch that pricks
the self conscious superiority
of those who speak for Christ?

Perhaps you prefer a world
where sensibility overrules sense
where patience has no place
where no one learns anything.

A cautionary tale about schooling in Australia

Acknowledging E.M. Forster's story 'The Machine Stops'

When asked about the view of the Principal of a metropolitan school who sees the school library and teacher librarian as redundant, a DECS spokeswoman said 'Schools are turning to computers'

We made the same mistake
decades ago deciding apprentices
were a cost not an investment.

So we taught children to feel
no joy in making, doing, growing
to turn up their noses and sneer at
those in heavy boots with grimy feet.

We taught them to feel superior
if their nails were clean, their skin
smooth, unwrinkled by sun and wind
and if their collars were white.

Someone else would clean up
after us, deal with all our shit, leave us
with our air fresheners and our
patterned, thick, white toilet paper.

Why did *we* need to care –
they would toil in thankless soil
get black grease in the pores
of face, hands and neck.

We, taxpaying voters, encouraged
to shrug off warnings about tomorrow
would rely on governments to import
those we were too cheap to teach.

Now we intend to do it again.
This hi-tech world with batteries
and power-plugs, rare minerals for
machines has use-by dates for all.

Made primarily to profit business
unlike those low-tech resources – books
that offer connections with imagination
without charges for cell-phone or PCs.

There'll be no room for age-old handicrafts
that teach children to appreciate textures
or value the skill that comes to fingers
with needle, thread, coloured cottons

making, repairing, even creating quilts
telling stories of life and love in families
providing patterns for children to explore
as they offer warmth to generations.

A hi-tech school will offer so little
so little to the senses, to taste or smell
or even touch beyond the smooth
surface of screens and key boards.

The hi-tech world is a reductive world –
reducing us to even less than before
without the need to feel or hear outside
this space, almost welded to these machines.

This is the sterile world that woman
that unknown departmental bureaucrat
supports – a world where there will be
even less need for people to be together.

And we will end up just like Vashti
in E.M. Forster's story *The Machine Stops*.
On an airship she is looking down.
'They were crossing a golden sea,
in which lay many small islands,
and one peninsula.
She reported, "No ideas here,"
and hid Greece behind a metal blind.'

Is it possible?

Will they no longer rub shoulders,
these books about myriad subjects,
tall, short, thick, thin, offering ideas,
voices describing, making commentaries
on so much outside our everyday world?

Will they no longer be there to take
a browser on a journey into the unknown
letting an inquisitive finger pick out a title
take the book to a table, check an index
make a note or pause to ponder a phrase?

Will the works of playwrights, poets, artists –
falling into the category of non-fiction –
be denied to students seeking other ways
of seeing, feeling, approaching topics
themes, subjects they must study?

Could it be possible that, here, in a school
or maybe in more than one school, we have
some Principals and School Councils eager
to follow the lead of the 'Terminator' that
former Governor of California?

That man saw libraries only as costs
decided to close them – everyone had machines
computers, the Internet, so there was no need
for them – individuals before their back lit screens
could save the State unnecessary expense.

It would be Ray Bradbury, author of that
Fahrenheit 451, the novel that took the burning
of books to a new and frightening level,
who would fight for those places of comfort,
combining learning and quiet companionship.

And school libraries begin the process
where children, students learn to seek
find, discover, share and talk together
not via some screen but face to face
in touch with worlds beyond their time.

Is it possible school governments might remove
The Math Book or *Grains of Mustard Seed* and
surprises in titles to force pupils to tackle aspects
of non-fiction, through screens in sedentary mode,
relying on a power source outside their own minds?

Exploring *The Search for Roots*

Primo Levi was asked to compile this personal anthology. In the Preface he wrote 'I accepted it as a bloodless experiment rather as one submits to a battery of tests because it is agreeable to experiment and to observe the effects.' He tells us that he 'came from a family for whom reading was an innocent and traditional vice, a gratifying habit, a mental exercise, an obligatory and compulsive way of killing time, and a sort of fairy wand bestowing wisdom'.

Could we search this way now in this new century
when reading is a chore bench-marked for literacy
when it is quantity of vocabulary not the singing
in the rhythm and the pleasure in the sound?

Will our children be able one day to look back
find the roots of their ideas, fears, hopes, dreams
in those books that gave new meaning to their lives
books that sparked or kindled another way of seeing?

At sixty-two this chemist, poet, essayist, novelist
this man for whom C.P. Snow's schism had no meaning
begins this task to find among all the books he has read
those thirty which have been 'essential reading,'

Before each contribution he tells why he thinks
he chose this work, why it is where it is but
he begins with a diagram, pathways, where he sets
authors from *The Book of Job* to *Black Holes*.

Rabelais will offer *Gargantua and Pantagruel* and
'Better to write of laughter than tears'. Carlo Porta,
'A Deadly Nip', Giuseppe Belli sonnets, and Sholem
    Aleichem
will provide pathways to *Salvation through Laughter.*

In T.S. Eliot he hears the simple women who know
suffering in the verse drama *Murder in the Cathedral* and
'Death Fugue' by Paul Celan he 'wears inside like a graft.'
Isaac Babel and Rigoni Stern complete this quartet.

This pathway of *Man suffering unjustly*, like every path,
starts with *Job* but next time a quintet will present us with
'The Stature of Man'. First Marco Polo's *Curious Merchant*
next Rosny's *Pact with the Mammoths*' and Joseph Conrad.

I rest here, recall *Heart of Darkness, The Secret Agent*
but for Primo Levi, it is 'A Testing Time' in *Youth* that marks
the stature of a twenty-year-old third officer in a decrepit boat –
followed by 'The Romance of Technology' in *Tugboat* by Roger Vercel.

And the ultimate connection in this quintet is Antoine de Saint-Exupéry
one who will die in war in the sky because he 'lived the adventure of flying,
like a new way of reading the universe'. But in *Survivors in the Sahara*
Primo Levi is not sure that he is 'on the button'. Still this work is here.

It is here with his chosen few. Not all thirty authors have a place on the path.
When we come to *Salvation through Knowledge* we return to a quartet –
first Lucretius' *On the Nature of the Universe*, next Charles Darwin with
'Why are Animals Beautiful?' Third comes Bragg. Then Arthur C. Clarke.

He is not last. All pathways, begun with Job's *The Just man Oppressed by Injustice*
come to this end. 'We are alone' in *The Search for Black Holes* by Kip S. Thorne,
the scientist at the heart of the 'cultural revolution being carried on in silence
by astrophysicists.' For Primo Levi we need to recognise that we are alone.

With Primo Levi's introduction to Kip Thorne we come to his ultimate question
'The misery of man has another face, one imprinted with nobility;
maybe we exist by chance, perhaps we are the sole instance of intelligence
in the universe, certainly we are immeasurably small, weak and alone but,
if the human mind has conceived Black Holes and dares to speculate on
what happened in the first moments of creation, why should it not know
how to conquer fear, poverty and grief?

Remembering an outstanding teacher

In honour of Kathleen Woodroofe, acknowledged in a PhD Scholarship in her name at the Australian National University. She believed in education as the true means of enriching our individual and collective lives.

It's nineteen fifty one –
we've passed all those damned exams
sat through stinking heat under the iron roof of
that jam-packed echoing showground pavilion,
with our talismans – crosses, sacred hearts, favourite
pens –
scratching heads, eyes straining for words we recognise
that will wake the memories and let them flow.

For three years straight we sweated there
and now we're here – we've passed –
we've passed and have the right to try
the right to climb those red brick stairs
with satchels, pads and fountain pens
and take that steeper path in
late summer's blazing days.

We've earnt the right to descend
to take the plunge and look down
into darker cooler depths of that
great Prince of Wales lecture theatre,
tramp down those steep wooden steps
to find a place on those steep curved tiers
far enough from that focal point below.

She's there – big, strong, corseted
immaculate, waiting, watching
as we come down, so many of us,
shifting along, chatting, finding friends
making room for them along our row.
Behind her on that great green screen
in faint chalk are so many names.

She waits – the shuffling slowly stops,
opened satchels are shut, pads are out,
pens ready – we're here to be informed.
That voice of hers reaches the furthest tier.
What are those words? There's not a single date
in British history. Not one word gives a clue
to where she's taking us.

But she's not 'taking us' anywhere –
we must work through these haphazard lists
and show what we know. But what is this?
Dreyfus, Zola, 'J'accuse' and *Germinal* ?
Einstein, Stravinsky, Diaghilev, Nijinsky
Clemenceau – we have heard of him –
Guernica, 'The Waste Land', Gertrude Stein?

And who's Max Planck?
What's that about 'The Blue Guitar'
and who on earth is Bertold Brecht,
Albert Schweitzer, Robert Oppenheimer,
Fritz Lang, the little tramp, Jean Cocteau?
And who is Jung? We've heard of Freud
but Shostakovich? Who is he?

And so much more – there's Florey –
we know him, he's ours and so is
Charles Kingsford Smith who flew
the Southern Cross – but who is
Eugene O'Neill and A.S. Neill and
do we need to know the name of
John Maynard Keynes?

Our faces tell the tale – there's fear.
For some indeed a 'wild surmise'.
All feelings of superiority disappear –
only one or two try not to look complacent.
I've got six right – that's not too bad.
We're being offered new connections
in ways we never imagined before
and some of us long to make a start.

Footnote: Kathleen Woodroofe was appointed as a lecturer in History at the University of Adelaide in 1951. I believe I might have been present at her first lecture.

In retrospect

At the first meeting of Friendly Street in the library of Flinders University

That Professor of English gave me a gift
when he denied me the right to do Honours
refusing on the grounds of a technicality.

They might do something for you up there
on the outer edge of suburbia in that place with
none of the traditions his Department prized.

They might take this older woman part time –
be prepared to test her out, make her work
see if she might be able to cross that divide

not that great divide, not the mighty chasm –
not that up hill climb beyond the lake to
those buildings with all those laboratories

just a little jump from history to literature
to a world that seemed to have no boundaries
where everything, anything, might be possible.

It would mean foregoing a different climb up
rungs of a narrow ladder of promotion and
taking another risk, part time, teaching boys.

Looking back I thank Professor Colmer.
I took his advice, began the climb, puffing, up
those cliffs to walk those brown brick corridors

to where Humphrey Tranter waited to take us
into the hearts and minds of English Romantic poets
saying my age made me cling to Keats' Ode 'To Autumn'

and where a quiet visitor from the Mid-West
would be there whenever I came just to chat
about Jonathan Edwards or Saul Bellow

and where Gene Le Mire would welcome me
when I strayed into that Victorian world
where 'ignorant armies clash by night'.

I had been given a place to converse and learn
where no one looked down on a woman who
just wanted the freedom to cross boundaries.

Listening to a woman of the New Guinea Highlands studying at Flinders University

High mountain ranges separate villages.
Women about to give birth hope
a midwife comes in time.

No roads for ambulances (if they exist)
and planes must make their way to
runways cut from mountainsides.

If there is a nurse or midwife or
a hospital a day away, will they,
mother and child, arrive in time?

And might they not prefer to stay
at home, on their land, where
they can feed themselves

saved from those extra costs
of rent, clothes, food and transport
even if they reach the town?

I listen to her, hear the courage
in a quiet voice daring to oppose
the power of the Catholic Church.

She'll support family planning
fight those priests who would rather
women die than use contraception.

Questions for Studio 131

The designers of the cover for Forward Thinking, *the collection of papers provided by speakers at the National Conference of the Australian College of Educators held in Melbourne, 21 June 2013*

In profile they face each other
one blue head, one red
without eyes to see
or ears to hear or
tongue, lips, teeth
to form words.

In profile, arrows red and blue
somewhere beneath the chin
suggest transference and
interaction but nowhere
nowhere near the neck –
far from vocal cords.

And where the brain might be
a jumble of incoherence
a red two plus two
becomes blue four.
Is this an exercise
in numeracy?

Equal signs connect no equations.
There's no symbol for trees though
the square root of one two three
is coloured green. Plus signs
add nothing. Minus signs
take nothing away.

And, of the alphabet, born from
words formed in childhood
no feeling for vowels or
consonants, no rhythm
in fact there is not
a single word.

Science is there in repeated symbols
we know from 'The Big Bang Theory'.
We are given H_2O but not CO_2
That's no surprise. No mouth
breathes in the oxygen and
no nostrils expel carbon.

Great cogs for machines, red and blue
fill much of the space but do not mesh.
Yellow screws, clocks for time
are stuck on nine. Hard to find
are signs for music but then
there are no ears to hear.

Could they find no symbols for
heart, hand and life? Were we just
to be content with science, maths
technology and engineering in
this jumble of disconnected
'Forward Thinking' signs?

Descartes' division of body from mind
is reinforced by all these abstractions
without links to ideas through metaphor
without song, without books or flowers
no hands or hearts to complement heads
no mouths to open and laugh.

If a picture is worth a thousand words
what do these designers say to us
to those who insist they believe
in education, who remind us that
tools are transitory, always change
and want us to focus on people?

In *The Professional Educator*, October 2013

The image accompanying the article – by John Quay, the opinion piece 'Educating the whole child: The dilemma of educational purpose'

Perhaps they are ready to learn from mistakes.
This time, the faintest curve for a cheek
this time from the black of the background
of the brain, the faintest grey for eyes,
nose, lips for this androgynous image.

This time clearer links in turquoise blue
possibly connecting across cultures.
A bird sings. There's a tick in a box,
an apple – well, it just might be fruit –
a book, bell, artist's palette and heart.

This time geometry, classical columns
musical notation, the double helix and
the mortar board. But she or he is alone.
The image must fit the page. No nerves
wake the senses. No muscles expand lungs.

And she or he is alone. Neither da Vinci's
nor Blake's connections of body and mind.
There is still no commitment to the whole.
No intensity of life. No cradle. No babe
in arms. The future is just in the head.

A second image in this October 2013 *Professional Educator*

Accompanying the article 'Educational purposes and the Melbourne Declaration' by Amy Chapman and Rachel Buchanan

Symbols are outside the skull this time
with its dark and light
of a single tone.

They are there without connections
floating in the ether – same old signs –
arrows, bells, computers, flasks.

But there in the back of that skull,
showing ears this time, only
different wheels.

No colour, no vitality, just
isolated. Yet they speak volumes
about today's educators.

Only the head – only the brain –
a stereotype, at that, just machinery
unconnected to the article.

Was this failure?

They said so. I had not met their demands. Writing in bed in hospital thinking on what that study of botany gave me I'm asking these questions.

A – Was it for adventitious roots of grasses or even the aerial roots of mangroves? Or the exciting idea of '*Avena fatua*' – wild oats!

B – What were the blessings of botany, enjoyment of field studies, and the life of bees, seeking nectar in blossoms?

C – Was it the names of a cup holding petals – the calyx for the corolla – and that word chlorophyll – and learning what the term meant?

D – Was it the dispersal of those seeds, some stuck as burrs on animals, others in bird droppings or blown on the wind like Father Christmas?

E – Was it the eucalypt here, the evergreen that, in England, took me to an ancient yew in a graveyard. Was it etiolation discovered in primary school?

F – Was it the fruit forming in the heart of flowers tickled by bees, even wasps in figs or wind-borne pollen between male and female trees.

G – Was it germination? That experiment on cottonwool with a broad bean seed to watch in water and light those signs of life – plumule up, radicle down to earth.

H – Was it a hybrid formed when cross-pollination occurred? Had I heard of Mendel then and his peas? My mother wanted purity in carnations!

I – Was it the indications of changes in the seasons, watched for in our plots of earth? Was it indications like bee-lines in flower or shoots from bulbs like iris?

J – Was it a juvenile plant growing into his or her adult form? Or other bulbs like jonquils? Did jacarandas speak to me then as they do now in their glory?

K – Why am I having trouble with 'K', wanting to tie it to the past? Not kiwi-fruit. Then I realise. Information has been becoming knowledge with that silent 'k'.

L – Well, 'L' was for legumes with the nitrogen nodules I saw when we pulled them from the ground and we discovered their role enriching the soil.

M – Many more 'Ls' came to mind – leaves, lichens, lithe lianas – but 'M' was there for manure and children who followed horse-drawn carts with spades.

N – Nitrogen returns and a memory of plants that close their leaves at night as well as lucerne, the legume, planted to revive great paddocks exhausted by wheat.

O – In hospital, it is observation, learning how to see, but now I can't leave out the extra oxygen I am receiving to breathe and want to thank the plant kingdom.

P – For photosynthesis, phonetically 'foto-synthesis'. So I shout about plants making food in light in the green of leaves. Recall that parasite – mistletoe.

Q – Is for questions as I write. Where is carbon dioxide? Was its absence in 1949 the reason I failed Leaving Botany? No one dares leave it out now!

R – Was it for the Rose Park Lorraine Lee roses on our fence giving their perfume to the breeze? Was it for respiration with plants breathing in and out through pores?

S – For seeds, flown, blown, caught, dropped – too many on stony ground. What else in an Anglican school with 'The sower' in the poetry of the King James' Bible.

T – Inevitably trees – native and exotic – and terms like schlerophyll for eucalypts protecting themselves from drought with the edge of leaves turned to the sun.

U – Is there anything with dawn coming as I sit up in bed building this alphabet? Six decades on I am awake to the unity of us all due to the greening of the earth.

V – Gives me variegated leaves and memories of experiments finding the starch, the food, in the green part – the infinite variety in textures, mosaics, shapes in leaves.

W – Demands on time – antibiotics – checks on oxygen in the blood so no 'W' but now, it is weather, seasons in our plots, of sun, rain, wind on our plants.

X – There is no 'X' except that this is Christmas Day and my Christmas Eve has taken me in this questioning direction, trying not to cheat with newer vocabulary.

Y – If I had reached this point, it would have been young life with memories of Field Naturalists taking me into the hills where I discovered my namesake by the verge.

Z – But 'Z' refuses to go away. Where has zygote come from? Did I know it then? Did it come later? What does it mean? I will go to my dictionary to find out.

All this if my breath comes as a sigh. All this if I practise and if I practise . . .

Reading as a child

The story is with me. I'm not down a rabbit hole not having tea with a mad hatter and sleepy dormouse.

Instead I'm in a termite mound. My name is Tessa.

My guide is Gilbert the Cricket, scientist and poet.

I am in two or three places at once
at one with Christopher Robin on that stair
half way up where we can be anywhere.

Here, down under, I return to Tessa
angry, kicking a stump, shattering homes
of white ants, seeking escape from school.

I become that country girl, hear a voice
offering freedom in a tiny different world
an exciting world if I eat these seeds.

It will not be a wonderland where flamingos
become the mallets for a game of croquet.
It will be a white ant world. Termitaria.

My guide, Gilbert the Cricket, singer,
scientist and poet, introduces me to termites
who eat my cotton dress, probe my white skin.

I am taken to their Queen, busy with babies,
am saved by soldiers repelling meat ant invaders
and more magic fern seeds let me return to my world.

The book is *The Magic Seeds or Tessa in Termitaria*
by Keith C. McKeown published by New Century Press Pty Ltd,
3 North York Street, Sydney, 1940.

A snapshot of Dorothy and Eric

The beginning of a family at Henley Beach with the birth of Erica for Eric and David for Dorothy

There is no photograph of him and her together
not even on the day they walked to the church
she, hatless, in that blue soft hand-knitted jacket
he in his suit, black tie, rounded starched white collar,
on that day they had waited for such a long time while
he, the youngest, caring for three of his older sisters
working for his older brother in partnership with
Strempel in that King William Street pharmacy
wanting to establish his own business near the shore
to pound mortar and pestle and fulfil prescriptions
sell ointment, calamine and sunburn cream to visitors
holiday makers brought by train from Broken Hill.
It would take six or seven years before that day arrived –
the day his ageing sisters lost their baby brother.

Later, was the absence of ceremony why she watched
other weddings, waiting outside to see a bride emerge
surrounded by families and friends – parents,
brothers, sisters, uncles, aunts, cousins, babies
ready with tubes of multi-coloured confetti
to pour over this radiant excited laughing couple?
Was this the reason she would refuse to move –
no matter how her daughter pushed or pulled –
looking at bouquets of white carnations, perhaps
blue forget-me-nots or tiny buds of Cecile Brunner?
And photographers, with Kodak or old Brownies
there to capture the anticipation in that new beginning
of man and wife so young at twenty-one or two
who would frame that reminder for their future.

There would be no photographs of smiling parents
holding the girl who decided to arrive six years on –
no fond father sharing with mother the joy in
parenthood. There never was a photograph of
them all together, not even when too soon
she handed him a son to make up for the girl
he had now learned to prize. He is not there
beside his wife who holds up their chubby baby
looking at her son with such joy in her face,
ignoring the girl, her father's name-sake,
standing beside her, smiling at the camera
eyes wide, a ribbon in her Curley-Petted hair.
But was he there, watching, admiring his family
and were her eyes on her father, not the camera?

Dorothy – at Rose Park

The widowed mother with her son and daughter

It delights me now she did not cut her pattern
to her cloth, never penny-pinched on books
or concerts, plays, opera, ballet, song,
refused advice that put the fear of debt
before pleasure in laughter and sorrow,
in those moments across the footlights
when all three of them roared at Roy Rene
laughed with Dick Bentley and cheered
when Gladys Moncrieff showed her
courage in *The Maid of the Mountains*
singing as if she was still young, as if
she was not held there by invisible ties
and feeling the sorrow when death came
in *Swan Lake* in Tchaikovsky's arms.

It delights me now she refused to listen to
advice on how to use the thousand pounds
paid by buyers for Eric's chemist shop.
Her children would not live beside that
row of low dwellings in Bowden, secure
since they would bring in rent as income.
It had been enough to live upstairs above
the shop when Eric climbed the stairs after
work or after that satisfying round of golf.
She had consulted the children's doctor.
He insisted Eric's children needed space
and space they would have with fine lawns
tall pines, goldfish ponds, a row of orange trees
and the perfume of Lorraine Lee at Rose Park.

The careful spinster sisters-in-law shook
their heads, predicting disaster for this woman
their youngest brother's spendthrift widow
but Eric's children were learning about style.
This splendid house with great bow windows
high ornamented ceilings and such space
gave room to play they had never known
on that balcony above the shop where they
rode their tricycles and scooters, watched
the world below, hoped for fine weather
to let them play in seaweed, build castles
or swim near the shore, safe in the knowledge
their father was nearby at work in his pharmacy.
With their mother, now, they entered her world.

Dorothy – in Hawthorn

War-time rent control would end her dream
of gracious life, taking away her splendid home
and Eric's children lost the school she had found
with the gentle Head Master she admired.
But he had been transferred and she would seek
a place where Eric's son and daughter could
be at his school, still have his kindly guidance.
No matter if the house was old, its southern wall
opening to the sky and letting possums in
her daughter's sleep-out, both of them could ride
to Westbourne Park and be with him while
she would take whatever work she could find
as returned soldiers took back their rightful place
and women, who had husbands, went back home.

Behind her wardrobe door that memory from
earlier years in her floor-length evening coat
rich, black, with scenes of nobility at play in
the Petit Trianon glowing in turquoise, gold,
silver and bronze as she swept into the foyer
of the Theatre Royal brought back the hopes
she once had and now had for their children.
How could she find a way to do her best
and satisfy her censorious sisters-in-law?
The Children's Hospital had an almoner.
The child psychologist would lead the way
discover their talents and their IQ levels
suggest directions for this next stage now
the peace time stage of secondary education.

And when the time came a promise was not
kept so, for Eric's son, there now would be
no future at his father's private college. Therefore
the nearby public Unley High had to be the place.
Its rigorous academic testing regime would not
do for the boy once snapped up there sitting
high up in a gum tree whistling to a magpie.
His mother would need to find another way
to release the talents of their son. It would take
the wages she earned and two more schools before
she could be sure he had enough to go ahead,
as he did, leaving to learn through work and life.
For their daughter, a scholarship opened the way
for the first woman in Eric's family to go to university.

Sleepers, Wake!

Acknowledging Barry Jones's book, from which I take this title while the Prime Minister, Tony Abbott, takes me back even further – sixty years

He talks like those self-righteous aunts of mine
but wasn't here during those post-war years
did not live with the memory of the Depression
reinforcing their refusal to consider investment
as the way to build a nation, justifying
their sneers and contempt for all in trouble,
those who did not, would not or could not
cut their pattern to their cloth, parroting
their sermon, 'Don't care was made to care'.
So often their niece grew tired and angry.
Refusing to spend more of her holidays with
the three of them, after she turned fifteen
she decided to free herself from their tut-tuts
doing their duty to their brother's children,
as they always did, while condemning their mother.

He sounds so like them, So does his Treasurer
talking of 'lifters' and 'leaners' to be discarded
as people 'without class' so often losing jobs
through no fault of their own as Dorothy did
when piece work ended at Viney's Copying Office.
That heavy Remington carriage had taken its toll
on her left shoulder as she pounded the keys
working at speed in this job her friend had found
to help her provide for her son and daughter.
Now, at fifty, she had to apply for a pension
not a pension for wives whose husbands gave
their lives in war, just for civilian widows.
Their snorts of contempt showed their disgust.
They had never, never, never taken charity.

I hear my fourteen year old self shouting.
'How dare you! My mother has paid taxes.
She has worked.' (As two of them never did.)
'All of us pay taxes. We are not seeking charity.
This is our right. We make our contribution.'
All my study of history and my study of civics
had been telling me about our rights as citizens.
(History was not an optional extra in those days.)
I knew enough to challenge those aunts of mine
and I thank them now. Their jeers and derision
woke me up to the terrible danger of their kind.
This Prime Minister probably sees such women
as the salt of the earth. When he uses that phrase as
praise we should know what salt can do to the earth.

Visit from a Great Grandmother beside the River Lee

For my great grandmother,
Margaret Mary Theresa Looney,
who came to me through stories from my mother, her granddaughter

She comes secretly in rumballs,
the thrilling conspiracy of grandmother
and granddaughter intoxicated by the
magic and mystery of theatre.

In that warm welcoming dark
both are free from drudgery and demands
by husband, children, mother, father to
let their spirits dance with 'Flora Dora'.

She comes to me in snippets of French,
sounds remembered, mouthed or sung by
her grand-daughter who brings with them
the 'je ne sais quoi' of her being.

She comes with scented petticoats
beneath rustling silk, unwilling
to give up those perfumes from Paris
in this dreary Melbournian exile.

She steals through the keyhole
of that bedroom door locked
against her husband each time
ships bring books from France.

She brings no baggage. Not one
of those thirteen children she bore
that Protestant tubercular husband
dares intrude on our meeting.

Certainly not her tightwad son,
eager to turn his widowed daughter
into his unpaid housekeeper for
the favour of sheltering us.

She brings, as yet, no legacy from Cork.
I hear no Shandon Bells beside the Lee.
Silent gulls swoop through mist
to its grey autumnal surface.

She is the bridge I would cross
to find that once bright-eyed mother
who brought her dancing spirit into
the dour existence of the Jollys.

‘And my poor fool is dead’

‘Prometheus was a fool’ said Ivan (Avalanche) Rehorek

I love fools
fools on the hill
fools, like Grock
bringing the sorrows
of the nineteen thirties
into the circus ring.

I love fools
feel the strength
in their fragility
take in the truths
they dare to speak
truths that cost their lives.

A Memory of John Bray

Acknowledging Wordsworth's epic 'The Prelude'
about a child's education

There was a time when life for me was hard –
power lay with one who lived by nothing
but 'the book', reciting every single part.
Where fountains once had played in air
now Wordsworth's 'dimpling cistern' took their place
capped their flow, forced back meandering streams
plugged creeks that dared to water dormant soil
beyond the borders of his pettifogging sway.

But I held on, scanning the morning waters
searching Holdfast Bay to find a sign –
an augury of joy to lift my heart
and fill my mind and hold my spirit high.
Pelicans or egrets, perhaps black swans at rest
would mark my way or feeding ibis
– sacred in the south as in the north –
to them in faintest hope I'd pray.

He could not know the liberty he'd bring.
Playfully I told our guest the auguries were good.
A white egret had crossed my path and flown ahead
along the Patawalonga way I took each day.

Head bowed this poet caught another tone.
Sharp correction rasped the voice of he who
knew priests consulted entrails of the dead.
He stood, this guest of ours, eyes hid beneath that
lowering brow and made a gruff reply,
a murmur loud enough to reach the pedant's ear.
'Romans sought omens also in the flight of birds.'
I listened, smiled, saw that principal give way
and for those timely words I thank John Bray.

A Moment of Madness at a Poetry Workshop

Being introduced to disassociation

A gust of wind blew out of nowhere.
Nowhere? Nowhere! *Erehwon*
by Samuel Butler
needed by John Bray
as a rhyme for subtler
in his 'Hymn to Chance'.

Come back wind and lift me
with a Mary Poppins' umbrella
somewhere, anywhere
beyond tomorrow.

Writing a Gallipoli Poem

The spark comes by e-mail –
for the theme of peace we'll be
bombarded by a battery of
cadets from Duntroon
assuring us soldiers
are peace-keepers.

My volley of return fire
results in a flanking attack
from a side-winder but
undeterred I open
the bomb-bay and
rain down words.

In a half-sleep state with
more words behind closed eyes
I find myself back in Gelibolu
that Turkish town so near
the peninsula and these words rise –
'This is a place to go alone.'

'Go alone' – not with politicians
seeking 'votes back home'.
Those 'o's – long, echoing
make me turn my hand
into a soft fist and
pound my pillow.

Now I hear the slow
muffled drum beat
and return in memory
to that day on that coast
and, at three am, a poem begins
with 'This is a place to go alone.'

A villanelle for JWH's disciple

How suitable this form for laissez-faire –
employers freed to do now as they please.
No pastoral pleasures for the workers there.

This French term – all workers should beware –
those with power can bring them to their knees.
How suitable this form for laissez-faire.

No out of bounds, no thought outside the square –
no extra payment and no more penalties.
No pastoral pleasures for the workers there.

Managers can rule, reject the need to care –
who dare question when a wage might freeze?
How suitable this form for laissez-faire.

Safe behind new laws, away from the glare
of frightened mortgagees, anxious families.
No pastoral pleasures for the workers there.

With less than a hundred, free to be unfair,
dismiss at will, ignore convention's niceties.
How suitable this form for laissez-faire –
No pastoral pleasures for the workers there.

After finding a 1953 music manuscript book

Thinking of Arnold Matters and acknowledging 'At night' by Sergei Rachmaninoff

I'm back in the front room
of that grey neo-Gothic building –
the Elder Conservatorium.

In front of me, near the piano
is that quietly-spoken teacher
holding a lighted candle.

He is teaching me control
helping me to keep shoulders down
and be at rest upon the earth.

If I follow where he leads
he will lift me from the ground
let me discover what it means to fly.

I must train my tongue
to lie relaxed, keep my larynx down
and free the pathway for air.

I read his notation, try the scales
remember the sounds and rhythms
he wrote out for me to learn

and as I learn to linger above that candle
keeping that glowing flame gently alive
I must let that breath come as a sigh.

My breath come as a sigh –
if I practise he will take me
to that world of German lieder.

I might be given the key to
a garden perfumed with linden trees or hear
a name float on the silent breath of night.

All this if my breath comes as a sigh.
All this if I practise and if I practise
I'll move a long way from jack-boots and rage.

The musician

He lifts me and on that current
air-borne though
planted here
I rise

only to plummet as
the G force strikes
the gut.

Yet I rise breathing, circling
in slow motion with
those strings that
pluck me up
again.

His fingers help me fly –
new thermals rise
and now I've
no desire to
look down.

A trinity to sing in your soul

Commissioned by a friend for her eightieth birthday and set to music by Anthony Hunt to be sung by St Peter's Cathedral Choir when her birthday was celebrated in the University of Adelaide's Elder Hall

Let me feel the states of being
there in the power of our earth
holding tight the roots of life

in sap rising against gravity to
branches and mosaics of leaves
shielding buds about to bloom

in aromas brought on a breeze
from eucalypt, boronia, jasmine
and the perfume of linden trees.

After seeing the new *Swan Lake* at the Festival Theatre, Adelaide

Take these tears to the world,
tears that rise, not from
unspoken moments when
eyes of women must turn away
afraid they might cry.

Take these tears to the world
tears that well and flow,
drawn upward by dancers
moving with such delight
there can be no containment.

Take these tears to the world,
tears that spring from beauty
on a stage, not rising from
silent conviction that we
must walk against war.

Share with the world these tears
of pride in performance, of arms
lyrical, liquid, lifting outstretched
hands to an audience so
rapt and wrapped in wonder.

Share with our world tears
of such boundless joy that
spellbound people hold their
collective breath only to
release that awestruck –
Aaaaaaaaahhhhhhhhhhhhh

Being alive

Nothing is
so intense,
so fulfilling
as expanding
one's lungs
being part
of a choir
and lifting
one's voice
to the sky.

Waking thoughts on whistling

for Michael Leunig

Wistfully he asked
'What's happened to whistling?'
to that light-hearted sound
swinging down the lane
filling spirits with joy.

I woke this morning,
heard Deanna Durbin
singing 'I love to whistle'
remembered Jiminy Cricket
tried to pucker up and blow

saw my brother
high on the branch
of a gum, looking up
lips pursed, answering
an unseen bird.

Fifty years on
after decades of
inhaling with
lips around
gaspers

a wheeze came
not a whistle and
those pursed lips
had little to do
with joy.

While not in the *Macquarie Dictionary*, in the *Oxford Dictionary* 'gasper' came into the English language in 1914 to describe a cheap cigarette.

Another reason to admire Ben Chifley

I faced this fear when, nine years ago,
I heard that worrying diagnosis –
emphysema.

My fear was real. I'd been invited
to go to see a friend's parents
in Vermont.

I'd seen the hole they'd cut in his throat
listened to the bubbling in that tube
heard him try to speak.

That man existed in that chair
an oxygen tank by his side
lucky he was not alone.

Could this be the future for me
coughing, struggling for breath
alone in one place?

Standing at the chemist's counter
presenting prescriptions for puffers and pills
I am glad I was not born in USA.

Born here, I'm the recipient of a gift
provided for this nation's public health
by Australia's Ben Chifley.

This post-war investment was made
when politicians did not frighten
voters with that word – tax!

More than fifty years on, I am safe
at least for now, from drug companies
indifferent to what I can afford.

And if, by chance, a coughing fit
sends me to a public hospital for treatment
no one, well not yet, will first check I'm insured.

A study in contrasts

Arising from time spent in The Queen Elizabeth Hospital

Each moment the possibility of drama
to be awake, steadily alert, aware
not precipitating, ready to respond.

It may be nothing. A steady calm
purposeful on shoes with quiet soles
voices cheerful, laughter among nurses.

So far from Sir William Upjohn
with his Rolls Royce, deep navy tie
caught with that startling diamond pin.

Matron beside him. Strong, self-assured
nurses in purest white, stiff, trim
marshalled to do him honour.

All this majesty and reverence
with none to gainsay his word –
and I felt the glory of it all.

This great man, this clinical surgeon
had been asked to relieve the cousin
from Adelaide of her piles – And he did!

Sixty years on. Another hospital
another place, another time
no grand parade – and I am glad.

I question, have the right to know,
not bound to take another's word
and doctors are expected to see me.

Not the patient. Me – the person –
unwilling to be 'she', unsatisfied
with the quip 'Ignorance is bliss'.

And everything I see and hear
tells me we were right when we said
maths, physics, chemistry are not enough.

A Visit to Centrelink

The reception desk is gone –
so is the queue.

She greets me almost
like a welcome guest
asks why I am there
offers me a seat
sits beside me
while I find the words.

I'm here to admit to
an infinitesimal rise
in my income.

'One of the lucky few,'
she says.

I feel the reprimand
accept the need to wait.

At a round table
are two sets of couples
waiting for a third.

No signs of poverty –
men's trousers regulation beige
shirts fashionably open-necked
designer leather belts and
clean imported shoes.

Their wives, knife pleated
linen textured slacks, cream
light coloured. Shirts or blouses
delicate colours, bright with beads
bling on wrists and bags.

Their chatter fills the space,
animated, quite at home,
conversation, laughter makes
this place their own.

Not long to wait –
an assistant comes, nods,
takes them to a private room
where I suspect they'll make
a case for increase in their
part pensions because
their shares have crashed.

Diagonally opposite
a mother, hair hidden
modest in the dark colour
of that voluminous dress
covering her from neck
to ankle and wrist.
Her slim teen-age son,
beside her – ready to
translate – is assured,
at home with his role.

They are collected
taken to a computer desk,
treated courteously
or so it seems from
where I sit and wait.

I'm left with two –
a young bare-footed girl,
hair badly dyed stares ahead.
With her right hand
she pats the shoulder
of the boy beside her,
the very thin boy beside her
dressed in fading black,
bent forward over his knees
his face hidden in his hands.

She, in her cerise camisole,
her midriff free of metal stud
is not cowed by this place.
A form is needed. He must sign.
Just before he goes to the desk
I see his face – skeletal, pallid, skin
grey at his young age.
She helps him sign, then stands
taking his arm as they leave.

After seeing Shostakovich's 'Leningrad' Symphony played by the Adelaide Symphony Orchestra to celebrate the close of a Festival

Waiting on stage
curls of wire and cords
almost hidden beneath a table
its sides draped with black velvet –
his instrument.

Behind the orchestra
demanding our focus
waiting for those images
and his interpretation –
three giant screens.

A visual artist
here *in real time*
brings something new
for us to experience.
We applaud his arrival.

A line of screens
tells him which images to
call up for which movement.
He presses keys, checks
his lap top, nods to music.

It's his chandelier
in the foyer of the palace
his upturned faces in the crowd
rapt in their united gaze at
benevolent 'Uncle Joe'.

He's here in real time
not in the reel time of
a projection room
hidden in some back wall
behind an auditorium.

Festival becomes fear.
Giant swastikas flank
a German eagle that
zooms towards us
overwhelming sound.

Flames on screens engulf
musicians on stage and
that crumbling city.
Time past and present –
his to command.

Do I want these distractions?
Teeth falling from gums
in the open mouth of
an old woman. Do I need
him to tell me the story?

A quiet movement
the slow motion of
delicate new green leaves
mesmeric, spell-binding
seduces me for a minute.

What am I missing?
Is it my freedom to
interpret swelling chords
insistent kettle drums
and crying strings?

Questions for the Director of *Queen Lear*

Did you expect placing the play in a 'mythical kingdom'
would ease your way, decreasing the complexity of the plot?

Is that why you left out the rulers competing for Cordelia's hand
Burgundy, wanting her dowry, the King of France, herself?

Were you deaf as well as blind to the line 'She is herself a dowry'
and the merit of the King of France eager to make her his Queen?

Was not Lear, as Kent reminded his Queen, insane to act in haste
dangerously mad, refusing to consider the costs for all her people?

Did you see just a senile, demanding old woman? Is that why the Fool
daring to speak truth to power, would become an inarticulate trio?

Did you put the Duke of Albany in that wheelchair to impress
on us his weakness, his physical weakness and his lack of valour?

Did you forget that Albany, when patriotism called, would act,
take charge and repel Cordelia's French forces at Dover?

So, when battle was joined, his English versus her allies, there was
no soldier, no guard, willing to take orders there for Edmund to pay.

There was no callous indifferent soldier eager for promotion
willing to accept Edmund's order to hang Lear's daughter.

What could you do? Who was on stage? Who could be used?
You made your decision and never thought about what it meant.

At no stage did you ever think about what it meant for the doctor,
calling for louder music to heal Cordelia's mother, to be the traitor.

Never, never, never, never once did you think what it meant for
Cordelia's physician, conveniently on stage, to take Edmund's bribe.

Did you not understand Shakespeare's firm intention to establish
the clearest line between compassion and callous, cruel indifference?

Remember Gloucester lost his eyes, had them torn out, for daring
to disobey 'the hot Duke' by showing compassion for his liege lady.

But you made Cordelia's physician as brutal and cruel as Cornwall –
the doctor, the healer, caring for his sovereign, would hang Lear's joy!

Why this interpretation?

To the Director after seeing The Three Sisters
at the Dunstan Playhouse in 2011

Did you think his world is past?
Is that why you pressed us down
with great slabs of grey concrete?

Is that why we had to go underground
to hollows dug out with great roots
winding through ancient passages?

Is that why we had to have
the presence of those men in
flannel shirts and baseball caps?

Was it essential for them with
their digital cameras to take shots
of this archaeological dig?

Here in Adelaide where so many
have longed and still long to be elsewhere
were Chekhov's sisters to be women of the past?

Were we meant with that pinboard
and photographs tacked at the back
to view the play just as a relic of Russia?

Was that ladder there for an actor
to rebel, climb out and leave the stage
through the door in that concrete wall?

What were we to feel leaving
with red dust raining down on everything
red dust steadily smothering everyone?

I left the theatre very afraid.
Could the day come when *King Lear*
might be presented to us as a fossil?

Acknowledgements

In appreciation of all those who made this publication possible

Making a Stand has grown out of my refusal to be silenced by those professional educators in academe and pre-tertiary institutions unwilling to make the much-needed effort to re-establish the connections between the sciences, the arts and the humanities. Past practical experience working with a number of fine teachers has shown me how effective such connections can be. So, in spite of lack of support, I have felt there is some recognition, in the practice of teaching, of the value of such interdisciplinary approaches.

In the acknowledgements in *Pomegranates* I concentrated on publications. Here I need to focus on the people who have helped me to reach this point. First it was three friends – artists and writers – Barbra Leslie, Elizabeth Mansutti and Tess Young. At Aldinga I introduced these friends of mine to each other in 1990. They understood my focus on connections and made me believe I had something worth saying but I had to find a way to do it.

My election to the Flinders University Council was the next opportunity. I was elected to represent graduates of the university. When the Council stopped electing a graduate representative the Vice Chancellor, Professor Ian Chubb, invited this outsider from secondary schools to join the Academic Senate. On the Senate I met Professor Ian Gibbins who, with Professor Marcello Costa, contributed to my effort to bring interdisciplinary engagement to the minds and hearts of teachers in the humanities and the sciences. Both scientists contributed to *Challenging the Divide: Approaches to Science and Poetry* which had short contributions by scientists to help students, and their teachers, see how scientists in different disciplines viewed the work they do. And, in some instances, they showed that scientists are poets too.

Being a member of the Senate allowed me to be involved with and to support the establishment of a most unlikely interdisciplinary educational institution – the Australian Science and Mathematics School, a public school. From the beginning it had a holistic philosophy. In the design there were no classrooms that could be isolated and cut off from one another. At the ASMS there were no separate, isolated faculty areas. In the design of the building, interdisciplinary faculties came together with no fourth wall separating them from the students. Faculty members could work in a collaborative way. They not only had the opportunity to work, talk, share, laugh, learn from each other; they have done so for more than a decade. They are still making all kinds of new interconnections across disciplines for staff and students, with so much being an adventure and I am grateful that I am still welcome there. And Associate Professor Susan Hyde has continued the support given by her predecessor.

Professor Chubb let me be part of that interdisciplinary collaborative advance in secondary education and I will always be grateful to him. I would see potential scientists talking about and studying history and literature. I could talk to a young girl about Beowulf the leader, not just the heroic killer of Grendel, but the leader who had to think strategically for all his people before sending warriors into battle.

My direct connection with that school was made possible by the Principal, Associate Professor Jim Davis and Terry O'Reilly, the Co-ordinator of the Interdisciplinary Curriculum/English and Humanities. Poems by students in Years 10 and 11 were central in Chapter Six of *Challenging the Divide*. We were proving that poetry had a place for students of the sciences and mathematics. Robyn

Williams, presenter of the ABC's *Science Show*, launched that book in South Australia's State Library in 2010.

I had written an article, *Poetry and Science in Education*, for the former Poets' Union. Prompted by *Accessing Australian Poetry: What Schools Need* by Warrick Wynne, it appeared in 'Five Bells' Summer 2005. That article had its foundation in the discussions I had been having about poetry and science with members of the U3A group at Port Adelaide. Those discussions had gone on for a decade from 1998. I would acknowledge their contribution to my research when *Challenging the Divide* was launched.

In October 2009 the Royal Institution Australia (RiAus) was established in Adelaide and housed in the former Stock Exchange now Science Exchange. Dr Lisa Bailey set up the science book club. It was important for me to read the books and take part in the discussions to find out how wide the 'chasm' was in the outlook of these lovers of science who joined the group. Even if *Challenging the Divide* failed to make a difference, I had to learn how seriously that 'two cultures' notion had affected the way these book club members saw the humanities. And it was good to be part of the group, set up by Dr George Aranda, senior science lecturer in the School of Education at Deakin University, who wanted to set up a similar science book club in Melbourne. Later, I was invited, when Friendly Street – Australia's first open poetry group – was cooperating with the RiAus, to join Sean Williams and Ian Gibbins to consider 'The War of the Worlds'. For a time the video was on the RiAus Youtube site. During a Festival after that meeting, my poem 'Michael's Cage', based on the work of scientist and visual artist, Judy Morris, about Michael Faraday, appeared on the red LED ribbon outside the Science Exchange which is now promoting sci-ku as a way of encouraging students to connect with science.

There appeared to be more evidence of the increasing

development of connections. In 2011 I was invited by Associate Professor Robert Phiddian of Flinders University to join other poets, among them Jude Aquilina and Ian Gibbins, to precede addresses by contributors to the Festival of Ideas. I felt honoured to be among that company. It seemed to me this was a sign that the 'times were a'changing' and I had hopes that teachers in schools might be coming to the party. In 2012 Ian Gibbins and I presented our poems about science at Poets at the Wall, the Treasury Wall of the State Library, organised by Friendly Street. Ian Gibbins – the neuro-scientist. Myself – a member of the humanities.

Throughout the period from 1993 to 2012 my poems, often about science, had been included in the annual 'The Best of Friendly Street' anthology. In all that time, the support of friends and academics who valued my efforts to encourage these connections kept me going. The former Vice Chancellor of Macquarie University, Professor Steven Schwartz, saw us as on the same path. He was trying to develop an undergraduate program in which science students took a humanities course and humanities students studied a science. In an e-mail to me he wrote, 'I strongly agree with the points you made in your letter, especially about closing the divide, but do not despair'. For a time an article of mine appeared on his blog. But, if teachers in schools and professors overseeing the writing of senior school syllabuses saw no value in the voices of Nobel Laureate Professor Roald Hoffmann, Nobel Laureate Professor Peter Doherty, Professor Jocelyn Bell Burnell and Professor Alan Lightman of MIT as well as Australian scientists sharing with students their love of science, and their engagement with poetry, what was I to do?

My friend, Ian Purcell, told me more of the same would not work. What about my own voice? I was unsure about that. In 1979 in an attempt to encourage English teachers to value connections and understand the need to recognise the fact that we write differently for different audiences, the late Frances Wells and I collected contributions for *Help Yourselves: An Anthology of contemporary writing on food.* The title was given to us by Phillip Adams. Contributors gave us essays about food or let us quote passages from their writings. We received contributions from Hugh Stretton, Iris Murdoch, Judah Waten, the Aboriginal poet Jack Davis, Robyn Williams, Howell Witt, Manning Clark, Max Harris, among others, as well as a valuable example of scientific journalism. Maureen Prichard illustrated the collection. The Director of Education, John Steinle, supported this not-for-profit publication. When teachers ignored this avenue of helping students to write for different audiences, the South Australian Department of Education pulped all the copies without telling the authors. What could my voice offer when teachers had shown no desire to read and share with students the ideas and words of such generous acknowledged authors?

But, in 2013 I had an exceptional opportunity provided by Margaret Sargent. Her willingness to accompany me let me do something that I thought was beyond me. (See 'Waking thoughts on whistling' for the reason why.) I could go to Europe one last time and fill myself with my loves and preoccupations. I could attend performances of Shakespeare's plays, including *All's Well That Ends Well*, and go back to the Natural History Museum in London. Margaret would go with me the first time and Tricia Bull, a friend in London, would go with me, get a wheel chair and take me back into the Cocoon in the Darwin Centre. The next day, Michael Bull would take me to Kew Gardens, wheel me everywhere and help me to find poetry – verses – among the shrubs. In addition, Margaret and I would see *Matilda*, the adaptation of Roald Dahl's novel for the stage with lyrics and music by Tim Minchin. Its laughing joyful assertion, in the face of the Matilda's horrid life at home, of the centrality of books and loving teachers and librarians and courage was what I needed.

In 2014, therefore, I took Ian Purcell's advice. Why not? What did I have to lose? With the inestimable support of my meticulous editor, who has edited my work for more than a decade, Dr Graham Rowlands, I decided to have a go. The trio who produced *Pomegranates* – Dr Michael Deves, Dr Maureen Prichard, Dr Graham Rowlands – have helped me to make this stand.

Friends assisting with research, as Mary Swenson has done with news cuttings, and those willing to listen to me have helped. They have put up with my fury, frustration and distress at the failure of curriculum writers, teachers and politicians to make the interdisciplinary re-connections that must be made to give Australia the scientifically-literate and humane citizenry it needs. So I thank them – Debbie Dixon, David Jolly, Dawn Langman, Reva and Michael Luscombe, Elizabeth Mansutti, Yvonne Miels, Louise Nicholas, Ian Purcell, Gillian and Michael Rogers and Jane Wilson.

But I am still not sure whether my voice will make any difference, so I complete this collection with a selection of references, voices of acknowledged scientists and other authors connecting the sciences and the humanities from the UK, USA and Australia. They are the voices of those who refuse to be set on one side of that so-called divide. They bring to their work the quality of emotion and intellect that rejects reductionism. They offer entry to the world they love in a way that Richard Fortey describes as 'an incitement to discovery'. Richard Fortey is a palaeontologist not afraid to bring the great theatrical director, Peter Brook, into his work. He uses this phrase in his Preface to *Trilobite: Eyewitness to Evolution.*

Erica Jolly
February 2015

Other Voices Connecting Science and the Humanities, with a Few for the Young

The ABC's Radio National programs *The Science Show* and *Ockham's Razor* – voices of knowledge.

Richard Aitken, *Seeds of Change: An Illustrated History of Adelaide Botanic Gardens*, Botanic Gardens, Adelaide, 2006. (See A.D. Hope's 'Australia'.)

Maya Angelou, *Poems*, Bantam Books, New York, 1986.

Natalie Angier, *The Canon: A Whirligig Tour of the Beautiful Basics of Science*, Houghton Mifflin Company, Boston, 2007.

Robyn Arianrhod, *Einstein's Heroes: Imagining the world through the language of mathematics*, University of Queensland Press, 2003.

Robyn Arianrhod, *Seduced by Logic: Emilie du Châtelet, Mary Somerville and the Newtonian Revolution*, University of Queensland Press, 2011.

Melvyn Bragg, *The Adventure of English: The biography of a language*, Sceptre, Hodder & Stoughton, London, 2004.

W.L. Bragg's Foreword/Introduction to T. R. Henn's *The Apple and the Spectroscope, being Lectures on Poetry designed (in the main) for science students*, Methuen & Co. Ltd, London. This edition 1967.

Quentin Bryce AC, CVO, *Back to Grassroots*, Boyer Lectures for the ABC, 2013.

Paul Collins, 'Rhyme and Reason: When formulae failed them, Victorian scientists turned to verse,' *New Scientist*, 23/31 December 2011 pp 58–59.

Suzanne Cory, *Survival on our small blue dot*, Boyer Lectures for the ABC, 2014.

Robert Crawford (Ed), *Contemporary poetry and contemporary science*, OUP, 2006.

Marcus du Sautoy, 'No more isolation,' *Oxford Today: The University Magazine*, Trinity Term, Volume 25, No. 2, 2013.

Rebecca Elson, *A Responsibility to Awe*, Oxford Poets, Carcenet Press Ltd, Manchester, 2001.

John Emsley, *Nature's Building Blocks: An A – Z guide to the elements*, Oxford University Press, 2001. (Look for 'the element of surprise' in each element.)

Patricia Fara, *Science: A Four Thousand Year History*, OUP, 2009.

Victoria Finlay, *Colour: Travels through the Paintbox*, Sceptre Paperback, 2002.

Tim Flannery, *The Weather Makers: The History and Future Impact of Climate Change*, Text Publishing, Melbourne, 2005.

Richard Fortey, *Life: A natural history of the first four billion years of life on earth*, American edition, Vintage Books, New York, 1999.

Ian Gibbins, *Urban Biology*, Friendly Street/Wakefield Press, Mile End, South Australia, 2012.

James Gleick, *The Information*, Fourth Estate, London, 2011.

John Gribbin, *The Universe. A Biography*, Penguin Books, London, 2008. (See also the work of John and Mary Gribbin.)

Susan Hall, *Ellis Rowan's Fairy World*, National Library of Australia, 2009. (For pre-school children. There are so many books encouraging these childhood connections.)

Christina Harrison, *Kew's Big Trees*, Royal Botanical Gardens, Kew, Richmond, Surrey, 2008.

Roald Hoffmann and Vivian Torrence, *Chemistry Imagined: Reflections on Science*, Smithsonian Institution Press, Washington and London, 1993. (His poetry is here too.)

Roald Hoffmann, *The Same and Not the Same*, Columbia University Press, New York, 1995. (See 'Fighting reductionism'.)

Miroslav Holub, (translated by David Young) 'Otters, Beavers and Me' in *Diseases, Politics and Other Human Conditions*, Milkweed Editions, Minneapolis, 1997.

Miroslav Holub, *Vanishing Lung Syndrome*, translated by David Young and Dana Habova, Oberlin College Press, 1990.

Joy N. Hulme, *Wild Fibonacci: Nature's Secret Code Revealed*, Tricycle Press, Berkeley, California, 2005. (For the young.)

Graham Jenkin, author, authenticated by Janis Koolmateri, *Meralte: The Boat. An epic story of the northern stars*, JB Publishing, Kurralta Park, South Australia, 2003.

Erica Jolly (Ed), *Challenging the Divide: Approaches to Science and Poetry*, Lythrum Press, Adelaide, 2010.

Barry Jones, *Sleepers, Wake: Technology and the future of work*, OUP, Melbourne, 1983.

Karl Kruszelnicki, *Science is golden*, Harper Collins, Australia, 2008.

Lewis H. Lapham – founder of *Lapham's Quarterly*. These focus on themes to bring us voices with different attitudes, outlooks, in time and place. He refuses to have a neat chronological order. They include prose and poetry. They cross disciplines, letting us hear voices over millennia.

Primo Levi, *The Search for Roots. A Personal Anthology.* Translated and with an introduction by Peter Forbes, Ivan R. Dee, Chicago. This edition 2001.

Alan Lightman, *A sense of the mysterious: Science and the Human Spirit*, Pantheon Books, New York, 2005.

Peter Macinnis, *Curious Minds: The Discoveries of Australian Naturalists*, National Library of Australia, 2012.

Peter Macinnis, *Rockets: Sulfur, 'Sputnik' and Scramjets*, Allen & Unwin, NSW, 2003.

Leonard Mlodinov, *Feynman's Rainbow: A Search for Beauty in Physics and Life*, Vintage Books, New York, 2011.

Jill Morris and Lynne Tracey, *Australian Owls – Frogmouths and Nightjars*, Greater Glider Productions, Maleny, Queensland, 1993. (Not just for young people.)

David Mortimer, *Magic Logic*, Puncher and Wattmann Poetry, Glebe, NSW, 2012.

Richard A. Muller, *Physics for Future Presidents: The Science Behind the Headlines*, W.W. Norton & Company paperback, New York, 2009.

Bill Neidjie, *Gagudju Man*, JB Publishing, Marlston, SA, 2002.

Martha C. Nussbaum, *Not for Profit: why democracy needs the humanities*, Princeton University Press, Princeton and Oxford, 2010.

Yoko Ogawa, *The Housekeeper and the Professor*, Vintage Books, London, 2010. (A novel connecting mathematics with lives.)

Naomi Oreskes and Erik M. Conway, *Merchants of Doubt: How a handful of scientists obscured the Truth of Issues of Tobacco and Global Warming*, Bloomsbury Press, New York, 2010.

Ruth Padel, 'The Science of poetry, the poetry of Science. Both depend on metaphor which is as crucial to scientific discovery as it is to lyric.' Guardian.co.uk, Friday 9 December 2011, pp. 1–7.

Bruce Pascoe, *Dark Emu. Black Seeds: Agriculture or Accident?* Magabala Books, Broome, WA, 2014.

Clifford A. Pickover, *The Math Book: From Pythagoras to the 57th dimension, 250 milestones in the History of Mathematics*, Sterling, New York, 2009.

Roy Porter, *Enlightenment: Britain and the creation of the modern world*, Allen Lane, The Penguin Press, London, 2000.

Gavin Pretor-Pinney, *The Wavewatcher's Companion*, Bloomsbury, London, 2010.

Kathleen Raine, 'The Underlying Unity: Nature and the Imagination' in *The Spirit of Science: From Experiment to Experience*, edited by David Lorimer, Continuum, New York, 1999, pp. 215–234.

Maurice Riordan and Jon Turney (Editors), *A Quark for Mister Mark: 101 poems about science*, Faber and Faber, London, 2000.

Michael Sims, *Apollo's Fire: A Day on Earth in Nature and Imagination*, Viking, New York, 2007.

C.P. Snow, *The Two Cultures and a Second Look*, Cambridge University Press, 1964.

Hugh Stretton, 'The Cult of Selfishness' in *Political Essays*, Georgian House, Melbourne. 1987.

Steven Strogatz, *The Joy of x: A Guided Tour of Mathematics from one to infinity*, Atlantic Books, London, 2012.

Lewis Thomas, *Medusa and the Snail: More notes of a biology watcher*, Allen Lane, London, 1979.

Sherry Turkle, *Alone Together: Why we expect more from technology and less from each other*, Basic books, New York, 2011.

Margaret Wertheim, *The Pearly Gates of Cyber Space: A History of Space from Dante to the Internet*, Doubleday, Sydney, 1999.

Judith Wright, *Collected Poems 1942–1985*, Angus & Robertson, Sydney,1994.

There are so many more voices making connections to help us to bring together the sciences, the humanities and the arts to help us, as C.P. Snow, says 'think with wisdom' for the future. We cannot undo the past but we need not go on reliving it.

I recommend you explore the International Lewis Thomas Prize for Writing about Science established by Rockefeller University in 1993. Richard Fortey was awarded that prize in 2003. His book, *Trilobite: Eyewitness to Evolution*, was short-listed for the Samuel Johnson Prize in 2001. In 2009 Richard Fortey was made a Fellow of the Royal Society for Literature. He has also written dinosaur poems for children.

The Samuel Johnson Prize is the British equivalent of the Lewis Thomas Prize in one way. But it is a non-fiction prize covering a wider range of subjects. Founded in 1999, in 2012 Alex Bellos won it for *Alex's Adventures in Numberland: Dispatches from the Wonderful World of Mathematics.*

The University of New South Wales Press publishes *The Best Australian Science Writing*. In 2013, poetry appeared in that anthology. The same has occurred in the 2014 publication with 'Firefront' by Ian Gibbins and 'Reached by committee, nineteen eighty-three' by Paul Magee.

Challenging the Divide: Approaches to Science and Poetry, has a bibliography covering a range of writing up to 2009. However, more and more writers make these connections and I keep updating them in a list of evidence of support for multi-disciplinary or interdisciplinary approaches.

My email address is ericajolly@internode.on.net

Wakefield Press is an independent publishing and distribution company based in Adelaide, South Australia. We love good stories and publish beautiful books. To see our full range of books, please visit our website at www.wakefieldpress.com.au where all titles are available for purchase. To keep up with our latest releases and news, subscribe to the *Wakefield Weekly* at https://mailchi.mp/wakefieldpress/subscribe

Find us!

Facebook: www.facebook.com/wakefield.press
Instagram: www.instagram.com/wakefieldpress

www.ingramcontent.com/pod-product-compliance
Ingram Content Group Australia Pty Ltd
76 Discovery Rd, Dandenong South VIC 3175, AU
AUHW011203281125
420182AU00010B/30

9 781743 053829